HOME BUSINESS RESOURCE GUIDE

by Cheryl Gorder

A guide to information to help start a home business and to find products for home businesses.

Includes:

Books for starting a home business
Courses for starting a home business
Wholesale products available to home businesses
Equipment and supplies used in home businesses

PLUS:

DIRECTORY OF HOME BUSINESSES

Reviews:

Booklist's Reference Books Bulletin (April 1, 1990)—"*Home Business Resource Guide* is a directory of information sources. The book includes an introduction to home businesses today, four thumbnail sketches of people working out of the home, and selected, annotated lists of information on starting or developing home businesses. ...*Home Business Resource Guide* is written for a popular audience and reflects traditional, home-based values."

Book Reader (March/April, 1990)—" ...a prime listing of names, descriptions, addresses, telephone numbers concerning all sorts of resources ... An enormous amount of information put together with care."

Also reviews by Small Press Book Review (May, June, 1990), Business Opportunities Digest, and Craft Marketing News.

HOME BUSINESS RESOURCE GUIDE

Published by:

BLUE BIRD PUBLISHING
1713 East Broadway #306
Tempe AZ 85282
(602) 968-4088

ISBN 0-933025-15-7
$11.95

Cover Design by Dale Gorder & Sarah Gorder
Cover art by Cheryl Gorder

Library of Congress Cataloging-in-Publication Data

Gorder, Cheryl, 1952-
Home business resource guide.

1. Home-based businesses--United States--Handbooks, manuals, etc. I. Title.
HD2336.U5G65 1989 658'.041 89-18205

TABLE OF CONTENTS

ACKNOWLEDGMENTS

Thanks to The Doula magazine for permission to reprint Jan Fletcher's comments on home businesses.

We appreciate permission from the NextStep Publications, (6340 34th Avenue SW, Seattle WA 98126) to reprint "Twenty Questions to Ask Yourself" which appeared in the book *Growing a Business; Raising a Family: Ideas and Inspiration for thw Work-at-Home Parent.*

Also thanks to Bob Anderson and Diane Washburn of Canvas Crafters, Dan Poynter of Para Publishing, Susanna and Donnie of Papa Don's Toys, and Coralee Smith Kern of the National Association for the Cottage Industry—for their interviews and photographs as successful home businesses.

ABOUT THIS BOOK

We have tried to make this book as useful as possible to people interested in starting a home business or to people who already have a home business but need additional information to help their business grow. Our intent is to include only legitimate businesses and business offers. We were not interested in any "get-rich-quick" schemes, so we spent plenty of time jurying the types of companies we included in this book. However, each reader should always investigate carefully each and every business opportunity that they are offered. We assume no liability to anyone with respect to contacts or negotiations which may result from the information in this book.

Please let us know about other businesses which should be listed in future editions of this book. We plan to let this guide grow along with the amazing home business trend. Also, if any negative encounters happen with companies listed within this book, we would appreciate hearing about them so that we can delete unworthy businesses.

We hope that this guide is useful to you, and happy home business!!

ABOUT THE AUTHOR

Cheryl Gorder's idea for this book came as a result of her work with homeschooling books. Homeschoolers are largely independent people with strong ideas about what life should be about. They generally live life according to their priorities, and one of their priorities is to spend time together as a family. Home business is a way to do this. As Frank and Sharan Barnett say in their wonderful book Working Together, home business is an end to separate lives and separate agendas.

Gorder's other books are Home Schools: An Alternative, which was on the Small Press Top 40 for 2 months in 1987; Who's Who in Antiques; Real Dakota; and Homeless: Without Addresses in America, which won a prestigious Benjamin Franklin award in 1989. Besides authoring books, she has edited others, including the Home Education Resource Guide, Spacedog's Best Friend, and I Was Homeless: I Know the Feeling. She is currently working on a social issues book and involved in finding solutions to this nation's homelessness problem.

1 out of every 7 businesses in the United States is a home business.

HOME BUSINESS AS A WAY OF LIFE

The number of home business in the United States has increased dramatically over the past fifteen years. In 1973, the Small Business Administration found that there were 2,500,000 home businesses. Ten years later, there were 5 million. And in 1988, there were 7 million. Estimates are that there will be more than 10 million by the year 1993. They are the largest growing segment of all businesses started in the United States.

Within the last two years, more than twenty new magazines have been published for the small business owner and entrepreneur. Many have more than 250,000 readers each!

Those figures don't even begin to count all of the people that are earning money from home businesses, because revenues generated from these businesses are spent in the community to buy supplies, equipment, and materials. Small business profits account for over $13 billion. Home businesses are generally found in households with an average income of $42,000. One in seven American businesses is a home business. The bottom line on home businesses is that billions and billions of dollars are earned by people working from home, spent in the community, and help other businesses.

What type of people start home businesses? There is wide variety of individuals who call "home" and "business" the same name. There is no one label that fits everyone. However, studies by the National Center for Policy Analysis in Dallas show that 70% of home-based businesses are run by women. These woman are generally white, married, and over 45 years old. But statistics are flat, not multi-dimensional like people.

People who run home businesses are a diverse group. They can be retirees starting a second occupation; middle-level managers who have been laid off; homemakers or child-raisers with extra time and energy on their hands; career women who have decided to be their own boss; blue-collar workers who want to start a business; or young people just starting out with idealism, enthusiasm, and a great project.

Whatever their background, home business people are individuals with an entrepreneurial spirit. They also have decided that the life they choose to lead is too important to be left in the hands of an uncaring boss or an impersonal corporation. "Quality of life is the prize they're chasing," said Thomas Miller, who directed a work a home study survey conducted by LINK Resources in New York City.

It's the ultimate dream of the Age of Aquarius dream of the 1960's—to do their own thing. People who have home businesses can set their own goals, their own hours, their own pace. It's an extension of the do-it-yourself trend noted years ago in the bestseller *Megatrends*. It's not at all unusual for home business people to be self-reliant in other areas. Many of them are home educating their children, with great success. Others grow their own food, build their own houses, make their own furniture, design and sew their own clothes.

In fact these things are some of the ways people build home businesses. Organic farms and herbal catalogs are an outgrowth of the trend towards healthier food and do-it-yourself projects. Log cabin home kits are often designed by small companies. Willow furniture is created and sold by craftsmen through catalogs and at Renaissance festivals. There are numerous home businesses that design and sell very unique and creative clothing. Home education has also become not only a lifestyle, but a business for many people. Raising a family not only can be very rewarding, but it can help generate ideas that ultimately become a product for helping other families.

A whole new concept of life is developed from living this way. It's called "whole life integration"—or making each facet of life significant and making sure each of a person's activities relate to the others. It means that life is no longer compartamentalized. Work, family, education, food, leisure-time activities, and social commitments must all follow the same values and incorporate those values in their day-to-day function.

People begin to listen to ideas such as cottage industries, homeschooling,

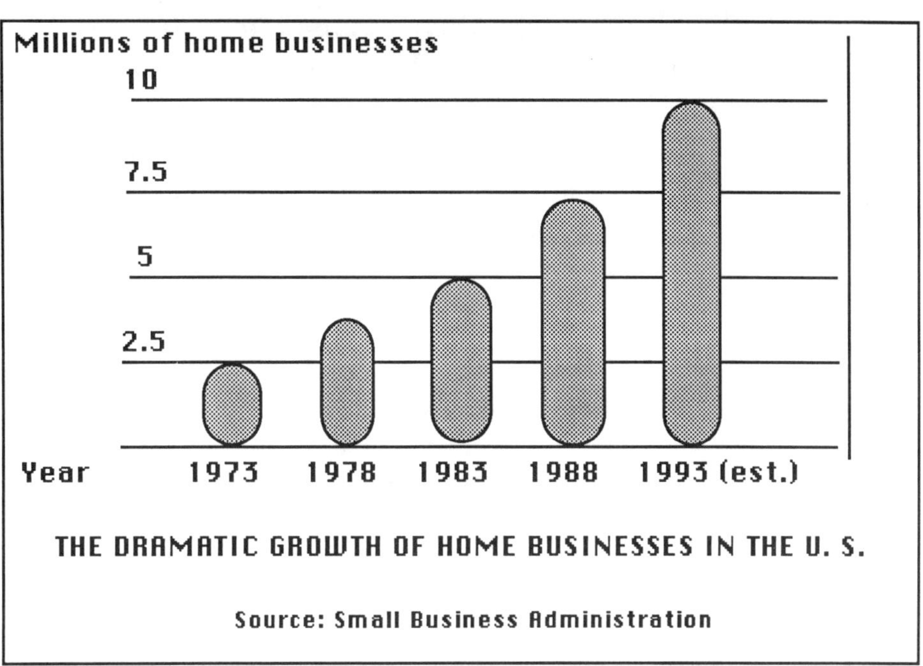

THE DRAMATIC GROWTH OF HOME BUSINESSES IN THE U. S.

Source: Small Business Administration

compassionate parenting, healthy food, clean environment, economic cooperatives, home computing, and alternative ways of living. Life begins to transcend money and material values. Accomplishment begins to mean payoffs in relationships as well as in finances. Success and knowledge take on a whole new meaning. Rewards are self-esteem for the whole family.

> "I think it's time for many of us to put out the welcome home sign for our husbands, our wives, our children, perhaps even our aging parents. It's time to stoke up the home fires, put the kettle on to boil, and sweep off the welcome mat. It's time to quit this commuting nonsense and go home.
>
> It's time to heal the wounds of the industrial age, time to clean up our messes, our pollution and our mistakes. Time to auto-

mate our factories, close our weapons plants, break up large farms into small ones, and bring our people home. Time to heal the emotional wounds of lifetimes of separation, to hug our children close to our breast and turn our homes into castles—places where dreams cast magical spells and we truly touch one another's souls through daily hours of living and sharing together.

It's time to come home."

—Jan Fletcher, reprinted from The Doula magazine, with permission

Home businesses are not only a way to earn a living, but they are a way of life.

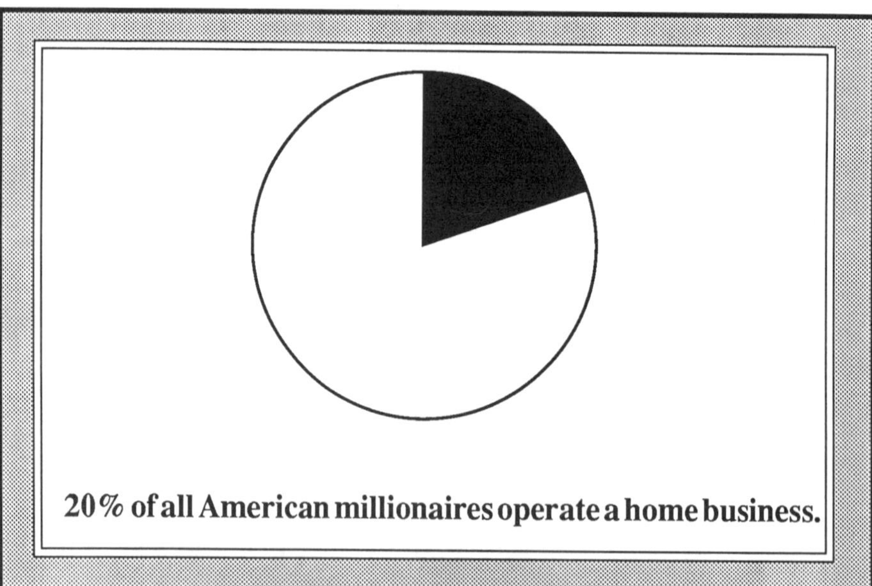

20% of all American millionaires operate a home business.

TWENTY QUESTIONS TO ASK YOURSELF

The following article is reprinted from the book *Growing a Business: Raising a Family: Ideas and Inspiration for the Work-at-Home Parent,* by permission from the publisher. This book is available for $9.95 postpaid from NextStep Publications, 6340 34th Avenue SW, Seattle WA 98126. NextStep Publications is also the publisher of the Home Business Advisor Newsletter, also listed in this book.

If you're starting from scratch and aren't even sure what kind of home business you want to start, this questionnaire may help you uncover the many factors which will ultimately determine just what business idea will work the best for you. This is a home business version of the old game, twenty questions. Have fun and you may uncover your heart's and your business' desire!

1. Do you envision yourself working part time (20 hours or less a week) or fulltime (30 hours or more per week)?

2. How much start-up capital do you have to invest in your business? (Figure at least two years before you will recoup this money, so don't invest something that you will need to have back before that time.)

3. Do you want to be working at home most of the time, or do you want a home business with limited travel? (for example attendance at craft shows, home parties, customer sales calls, etc.)

4. Do you have a particular skill that you want to pursue? (typing, crafts, writing,

baking, child-care, etc.)

5. How much physical space can you devote to your business? (spare room, basement, closet, or entire floor)

6. Will your home owner's policy and zoning laws provide adequate provisions for your business ideas?

7. Will your children participate in your business? What are their feelings about it? If they are older than three, you will need to take their feelings into consideration. If they are younger than three, you need to consider what their present routine is and how your business plans will affect them.

8. How does your spouse or partner feel about your business plans? Will he/she provide any assistance? Will he/she join your business later as a fulltime partner? Will his/her present job help support your business and your family until it gets off the ground?

9. How much money do you want to make from your business?

10. How important are the following motivations in your business plans? Rate each one on a scale of one to 5 with five being the most important:

❑ income
❑ using your work to education your children and involve them in your business
❑ building up a business so that it will eventually support your family fulltime
❑ gaining experience in a new field
❑ working together with your spouse in a family business
❑ being with your children for most of the time
❑ being available for your children but still having several hours a day when they are with someone else or at school
❑ occupying your time with productive enterprise

- ❑ stimulating work
- ❑ working independently and by yourself
- ❑ having regular contact with others
- ❑ keeping proficient in your chosen field while being at home with your children

Consider your answers to these questions and compare them with business ideas that you are considering. Be cautious if any serious conflicts reveal themselves, because you don't want to start a business that goes against something that you consider important to the overall well-being of yourself and your family.

11. Will you need regular transportation? How big will your vehicle have to be?

12. How much equipment do you already have that you can put to use in your business? (phone, office equipment, books, furniture, vehicles, computer, etc.)

13. When do you want to start your business? As soon as possible, or can you wait a year?

14. How much preparation time will you need? (prep time includes research, product development, etc.)

15. What kind of previous work experience have you had that you can apply to a home business?

16. Do you want a partner (including your spouse of life-partner)?

17. Do you want to turn a volunteer activity into a paid activity?

18. Do you want hours as flexible as possible or would you mind structuring your work time similar to a standard work wee?

19. Do you care about how you dress and what your office looks like? (Matters little

in mail-order, matters a lot in teaching or consulting work.)

20. Where would you like to be as a family and in your career five years from now?

Did you know—

✔That there are over 7 million home businesses in the US?
✔That 1 in 7 American businesses is a home business?
✔That 20% of all American millionaires run a home business?
✔That 70% of all home businesses are run by women?

HOME BUSINESS PROFILES

A LOOK AT SOME SUCCESSFUL HOME BUSINESSES AND THE PEOPLE WHO OWN THEM.

Above: Canvas Crafters building at the Arizona Renaissance Festival, which Bob designed himself and built with his brother in only 14 days.

Left: Child-size canvas chair.

CANVAS CRAFTERS:
The Simplest Things Are Best

The most romantic lifestyle in America today is the one that real kings, queens, courtiers, jesters, henchmen and knights would envy. That is, the Renaissance Festivals. Each festival is a recreation of a European village during the 14th to 16th centuries, the Renaissance period. It's a trip back four hundred years to an era before nuclear weapons, before electricity, and before the pressures of the modern world. It's a unique place for actors to stretch their skills, and a unique niche for craftsman to sell their wares.

It was at one of these Renaissance Festivals that I discovered Diane Washburn and Bob Anderson. They own Canvas Crafters of Boulder, Colorado, and sell their products at booths in Renaissance Festivals across the nation.

Their product is a great hanging canvas chair. The chairs won first place in an International Canvas Furniture Design Competition. They are carefully crafted with quality materials and can be hung from a ceiling joists or outside from a porch rafter or from a tree branch. The chair is fully adjustable and comes ready to hang with hooks included.

Bob and Diane didn't start out in life with a canvas chair business. Diane received a degree in elementary education and sociology, and Bob was involved with woodworking. Diane's cousin Kurt Buetow originally designed the chair while at Experimental College at the University of Minnesota. He entered the chair in the International Canvas Furniture Design Competition in Tokyo in 1974. When he found out that the chair was one of ten finalists, he went to Japan, and returned with 3 million yen (about $10,000) first prize money.

Above: Bob sewing canvas chairs. They no longer use treadle machines or sew by the light of kerosene.

Left: The trusty bus that took them all around the United States to Renaissance Festivals and craft shows.

With the prize money and the award as incentive, Kurt went to backwoods Wisconsin and started making more chairs. Soon Diane and Bob were involved as well. The first chairs were made by treadle sewing machines in a shop that had no phone, water, or electricity. Many nights they sewed the canvas by the light of kerosene. Everything was hand-dyed, and since there was no running water, the water used for dyeing had to hauled from the creek or melted from snow over the wood stove. The wooden dowels were hand-cut saplings.

"We had no idea the chairs would be so successful. It caused us to change directions in ways we hadn't anticipated."

People loved these wonderful chairs from the start, and were telling Bob and Diane that they ought to exhibit them at the Minnesota Renaissance Festival, near Shakopee, Minnesota. In 1977, these types of fairs were relatively new, but they decided to give it a try.

Their first Renaissance Festival weekend was so successful that they sold out of chairs. In order to have any chairs for the next weekend, they rushed mid-week to Kansas City, bought dyed canvas, rushed back to Minnesota, and made more chairs for the next weekend.

The Renaissance Festival proved to be the start of something big. Diane said, "We had no idea the chairs would be so successful. It caused us to change directions in ways we hadn't anticipated."

The next year they participated in three Renaissance Festivals, including the giant Texas Renaissance Festival. Year by year, they increased the number of festivals they were attending, and added arts and crafts shows. Their third year they bought a bus to convert into a motorhome for living on the road while attending these shows. They took out all of the seats, installed a shower and closets, put a workshop in the back, and had a bench that turned into a bed.

Living in the bus while traveling from festival to festival proved to be very good for them. Not only was their workshop always with them, but they were able to live meagerly and save lots of money. Winters they spent in Tucson or in Europe.

The success of the chairs plus the inexpensive lifestyle resulted in enough savings so that now they have a home in Boulder plus a cabin in the mountains of Colorado. Although they still participate in Renaissance Festivals, they are more likely to fly in and fly out rather than drive the bus. That's because they are also very busy with mail order sales. They have a toll-free order number in Boulder, and their chairs can also be found at an arts cooperative in Boulder.

"It's basically a simple design... but sometimes the simple things in life are best."

Although they no longer need to cut saplings or hand-dye the canvas, their chairs are still made of quality materials, such as ash dowels from Maine. The design of the chairs attracts people because of three very important elements: comfort, color, and cost. People say it's like "sitting on air" and that sitting in them can become addictive. Bob says, "It's basically a simple design...but sometimes the simple things in life are best."

For Diane and Bob, these simple things are not only the best, but they are a way of life.

Canvas Crafters
1705 14th Street #122
Boulder CO 80302
(303) 494-3807
Toll-free order number 1-800-365-1199
VISA/MasterCard orders accepted

In Boulder: Arts Crafts Cooperative
1421 Pearl Street

DAN POYNTER: PARA PUBLISHING
The Three Million Dollar Man

Thousands of people have learned how to become publishers from just one man: Dan Poynter. He is single-handedly responsible for teaching successful publishing through his books, seminars, reports, newsletter, and private consultations. His name is synonymous with independent publishing.

He is the author of 29 books, 16 special reports, and over 500 magazine articles. Everywhere you look in the publishing world, you see his name and his fame. Self publishers consider him the leading authority on the subject.

His home-based company, Para Publishing of Santa Barbara, California, has sold over $3 million and over 500,000 books in 17 years of self-publishing. His success has provided him with a hilltop home near Santa Barbara that overlooks the Pacific Ocean and has a view of the Channel Islands.

Like many successful entrepreneurs, Dan Poynter did not plan to do what he is so successful at today. He was "trying to find himself" during his six years at six different colleges. He spent two years in law school. Then, while studying for finals at law school, a friend said they should try a parachute jump.

After just one jump, Dan was hooked. He called it "the most exciting thing ever." Thereafter he centered his life around parachuting, becoming a manager of a parachute loft in Oakland, California. He became a parachutist expert as jumper, instructor, rigger, pilot, rescuer, inventor, witness, and executive for parachute associations. This led to his position as a design specialist and marketing manager for a parachute company in Massachusetts. Interestingly enough, this company was in the mail order business, which taught him many of the skills he would later use in his own

Dan Poynter
Para Publishing

company.

His expertise in the field led him to start writing about parachuting in 1963. He had a monthly column in *Parachutist Magazine* and wrote numerous articles. Although it was a non-paying job, it did help him develop research and writing skills, plus he accumulated a wealth of material on parachuting.

"I would much rather be a has been than a never was!"

Eventually he decided to use this volume of material to write a book. It was an enormous project, but he was learning organizational skills that later helped him construct other books. The result was the 1972 book *The Parachute Manual,* a comprehensive 600-page book with 2,000 illustrations. The book has been revised twice over the years and is still in print. He still sells 1,000 copies a year at $45 each and 16,000 copies have been sold.

Thus Para Publishing was born. Why did he decide to self-publish? Dan says, "Why ship your manuscript off to New York, when you can give it to a printer and be on the shelves in a month or two? ....Another important consideration is why settle for a 10% royalty when you can have it all?"

The economic advantages of self-publishing are enormous. A writer generally receives a standard royalty of 6% to 10% of net sales of the book, but a publisher receives about 40%. In other figures, an author earns about 50¢ per book and a publisher earns about $4 per copy. A well-promoted title with a broad appeal has an open-ended limit to sales. Many books by independent publishers keep on selling year after year after year.

In 1973, Dan became excited about hang gliding. Since he could not find anything in the library about the sport, he once again self-published a book, *Hang Gliding: The Basic Handbook of Skysurfing*. It was an instant success. There are now over 130,000 copies in print.

Dan's first love—parachuting—did eventually lead to painful and expensive injuries. He was also injured while hang gliding. He has retired from active skydiving, but as he says, "I would much rather be a has been than a never was!"

The sports left him with more than just memories, because they led him to his successful business as a publisher. After his very popular parachuting and hang gliding books, he produced a *Frisbee Players Handbook,* which has Wham-O, the Frisbee manufacturer, as its biggest customer. It is a very unique book in that it has a round shape, so that it could be nested and shrinkwrapped into a Frisbee disc. That book has sold over 25,000 copies and has even been translated into Japanese.

By this time, many people recognized his self-publishing successes and approached him for their own books. That led Dan to write *The Self-Publishing Manual,* which has been said to have launched a thousand books and has been a godfather to many more. Dan says of the book, "It was a book that needed to be written. It was a book I just had to write! ...I had the background and the information; a book was the most logical format to market and distribute that information."

It was a book that needed to be written...It was a book I just had to write!

That book not only told people how to write a book, how to organize it, and how to produce it; it also told them how to sell it! It was an incredible step-by-step guide in an area that was really needed. Thousands of good manuscripts were going by the wayside because of the lack of interest or the lack of time, (or whatever) of major publishers. This book, along with the computer technology revolution, sparked much of today's desktop publishing.

The book made him the guru of independent publishing, and made Para Publishing the central headquarters. The company now sells everything a person needs to become a publisher. Other titles include *Is There a Book Inside You?* and *Publishing Short-Run Books.* In addition to his own books, he has developed an "Author/ Publisher Bookshelf" of selected titles from other companies. He has a line of reports that are also very informative and keep publishers up-to-date with current marketing and technology information.

Dan opens his home five times a year for detailed seminars on publishing. The reason he is so helpful is not only because he shows shortcuts that save publishers

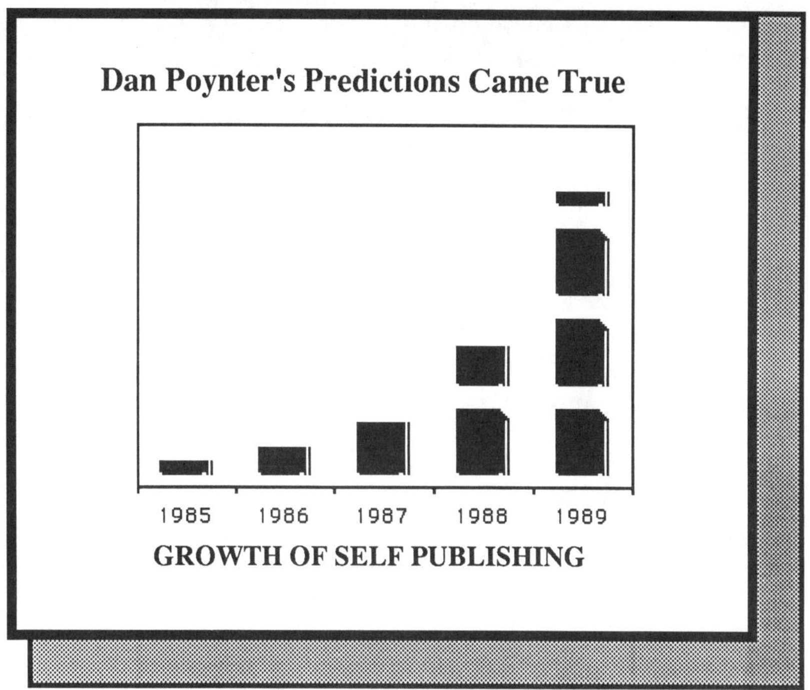

thousands of dollars in producing a book, but primarily because he is such a whiz at marketing books.

Independent publishers sell only 10% of their books to bookstores, so there's a great deal of creativity involved in selling the other 90%. That's where Mr. Poynter has really evolved beyond most publishers, and why his skills are so useful. He knows how to tap into unusual markets for books, and how to keep sales rolling.

Mr. Poynter said four years ago that "self-published books will double in the next six months, quadruple in the next year and a half" and they did! Self-publishing is the hottest growth segment in the publishing industry, and Dan says it's because it's the most imaginative.

When asked if he recommends operating a publishing business out of one's home, he said, "For many people it is the ideal set up. The commute is short; the hours are flexible and the tax breaks are better....It takes organization, discipline and a little imagination but working like this provides a no-stress atmosphere."

Self-publishing appears to be one of the best home businesses available in terms of work conditions, flexibility, and financial potential. To learn more, be sure to write to Dan and ask for his free brochure. "Book Publishing Resources from Dan Poynter".

Para Publishing
PO Box 4232
Santa Barbara CA 93140-4232
(805) 968-7277.
Toll-free for orders 1-800-PARAPUB

PAPA DON'S TOYS
"Quality Hardwood Toys Made Fresh Daily"

Little did Susanna and Donnie know that the little wooden rattle Donnie made for their infant daughter would end up bringing them such success. Sixteen years later, that little rattle has resulted in a nice big factory, a house, land, and all the comforts they could ever ask for.

Of course, we know that the rattle alone is not responsible for all of that. It actually takes persistence, dedication, and lots of old-fashioned hard work. The fact is that Donnie and Susanna found a product that they believed in, and stuck with it.

After Donnie made their baby daughter that first rattle, he made a few more, which they took to a local market to sell. Susanna said that immediately "the response was real positive." So they made more rattles, plus designed more toys. At first they were working in their garage and a small workshop. They would design new toys and then take them out to sell. If the product caught the public's attention, then they made more. If it did not, then they would change it or just shelve the idea for a while. They found that some of their designs were ahead of their time, and that products they shelved ten years ago are now very much in demand.

They kept expanding their woodworking tools and skills as the business grew. If they saw a wooden product that had an idea or part that they could use, but they weren't sure how it was done, they asked questions, plenty of questions. Through the questions and through lots of trial and error, they became self-educated in woodworking skills.

They continued attending arts and crafts markets with the toys, and working tremendous hours. Sometimes on a weekend, Susanna would set up at one

Susanna & Donnie

crafts show and Donnie would attend another. Susanna said, "At first we worked very hard. We were working seven days a week, sacrificing a lot to get where we're at now. It took seven years for the business to get to where it was easy. It was well worth it, though, because there was a lot of excitement along the way."

As the business grew, it changed in directions according to the wishes of the public. The designs or concepts of the toys would change according to the feedback from the customers. And the public started demanding that they wholesale the products, as well as sell by mail order. Susanna noted that, "Everything we've done has been in response to what people want. We were wholesaling by the third year."

Now the bulk of their business is wholesale. They produce the toys with three employees, working three to five days a week, according to their production needs. They still attend arts and crafts shows all over the West Coast, because they find that they need the public feedback in order to keep their ideas fresh. Besides, they enjoy those shows.

They have kept the business to the size that they want. It's just big enough to generate income for anything they want or need,but small enough that they don't have to work fulltime. They have enough time to spend on other interests in their lives.

A FAMILY OWNED BUSINESS

QUALITY HARDWOOD TOYS
MADE FRESH DAILY

SINCE 1973

Walker Creek Road • Walton, Oregon 97490 • (503) 935-7604

"Enjoy what you are doing. Do not be motivated just by profit."

Susanna said, "We have kept it small intentionally. If we ever got the urge to expand and grow, we could. Right now it pretty much runs itself and is not very demanding."

Having a home business was good for their family, they believe. Because when the kids were little, there were always both parents home together. The travelling was also good for the kids. It provided enjoyable times together as a family, and unique experiences for the children.

Susanna and Donnie have always had very strong ideas about what life is supposed to be like, and they have lived according to their priorities. They have always tithed 10% of their income, even at first when that income was very meager. They believe that somehow that tithing and sharing with others is one of the reasons that toymaking "has been a real blessing for us."

They have excellent advice for others starting a home business. "Enjoy what you are doing. Have a good feeling about what you are offering. Do not be motivated just by profit."

They also emphasize that your product should be something that the public wants and can afford, yet still generates a profit for you. They warn that, "Artistic people sometimes get attached to what they are making and become inflexible. Don't be inflexible. Give the public what they want."

Another very important hint that they offer is, "Keep growing and changing. Stagnation is detrimental."

Donnie and Susanna have achieved the kind of life they always wanted. They have done it by hard work and persistence, and also by doing something they truly believed in. As for the material rewards that came with a successful business, they say, "We earned it." There's nothing better than that!

Papa Don's Toys
Walker Creek Road
Walton OR 97490
(503) 935-7604

CORALEE SMITH KERN
Champion for Home Businesses

One of the most outspoken advocates for home businesses is Coralee Smith Kern. She has been very active in speaking out for protective legislation for home businesses. Her reasons for doing this work are based largely on her own experiences. Twenty years ago, when she was ill for a long period of time, she started a business from her home. This home business enabled her to have an income in spite of her poor health. “It was a godsend,” she said. “I really believe in the whole concept of home business."

The business she started in 1970 was Maid-to-Order, Inc., which has grown from a 2- to a 460-employee company providing maid and party service for the Chicago area. In 1984 she wrote Maid to Order: A Package for Success, a book relating her advice on how to start an operation similar to her own.

Her strong interest in home business soon led her to form the National Association for the Cottage Industry, which became an important clearinghouse of information for homebased cottage industries. The organization’s newsletter “Cottage Connection” is the watchdog on legal updates for cottage industries. Recent issues have published responses to her letters from various states’ Department of Labor regarding their laws on “home work” and “cottage industry”.

As the executive director of the NACI, Coralee has directed highly successful regional conferences which have been co-sponsored by the US Small Business Adminstration. She said, “We have received inquiries from many people who have been displaced or terminated from their regular employment and realize a home occupation is their best solution for income. These are the people whom we want to help.”

For a number of years, Mrs. Kern has conducted seminars and workshops that provide first-hand problem solving and allow men and women to explore new home business opportunities as well as meet others who have homebased businesses. In October, 1989, she organized a Home Business Show in Chicago, at which there were speakers and exhibits.

Coralee Kern

Coralee is highly visible in the world of home business, and as such has used her influence to try to persuade lawmakers to repeal laws that are harmful to cottage industries. "But it isn't going to be easy for us until we can prove to city and town officials we are not a threat but a legitimate and worthwhile addition to the economy of our country," she said. "There is no question we should be subjected to the same rules and regulations as the rest of the business community, but as long as we do not change the character of our neighborhood, we should be allowed to work from our home base."

Her personal philosophy of home business is that "clearly working from home is a lifestyle choice and not just a financial choice" but "there is no doubt that one's own business can be successful."

Coralee will keep being a champion for the cottage industry, as the cottage industry has been a champion for her.

Coralee Smith Kern
c/o National Association for the Cottage Industry
PO Box 14850
Chicago IL 60614
(312) 472-8116

DIRECTORY

BOOKS

Aames-Allen Publishing, 1106 Main St., Huntington Beach CA 92648-2719. (714) 536-4926. *Word Processing Profits at Home* by Peggy Glenn. One of the most popular books about starting a computer-based word processing business at home. Packed full of information and good advice. Includes hints for markets, advertising, publicity, customer relations, and more. 210 pages, $15.95 postpaid. Also *How to Start and Run a Successful Home Typing Business* by Peggy Glenn. Covers every detail of a home typing business and how to get clients. $15.95 postpaid. These two books are considered standard manuals for these types of businesses and are a must if typing or word processing is what you are considering for a home business.

Acropolis Books, Ltd., 2400 17th St., NW, Washington DC 20009. (202) 387-6805. This company has several books that will be helpful to the home business person. The first is *Image Consulting: The New Career: How to Build an Exciting Money-making Career on Your Own Time* by Joan Timberlake. This is a step-by-step guide to becoming an self-employed image consultant. Just what is an image consultant? A person who helps advice clients on fashion, color choices for make-up and clothing, and helps develop a public image for the client. The author explains how this successful, yet flexible career can begin part-time out of the home and grow into any proportions you're capable of handling. Once you have developed a clientele, you can train others and branch out. 159 pages, $8.95.

Making It On Your Own by Dr. S. Norman Feingold and Dr. Leonard G. Perlman. Be your own boss and become the master of your own destiny by having your own business. This book helps you find the business that fits you and tells you how to take the first steps. 30 pages, $7.95.

America's New Breed of Entrepreneurs: Their Marketing Strategies, Techniques, and Successes by Jeffrey L. Seglin. A book that explains the six maxims of entrepreneurial marketing that keeps them leaders in their marketplace. Uses examples from current successful businesses. 272 pages, $8.95.

Sell Like a Pro by Sherrill Y. Estes. Every type of business involves some type of selling, whether it be selling your service or selling your products or selling your idea. So learning how to sell like the experts is a very good idea. For instance, what negative words to avoid are explained in the book. And how to ask questions properly to make the sale without offending the buyer. Very practical advice. 192 pages, hardcover, $18.95.

Barbara Brabec Productions, PO Box 2137, Naperville IL 60566. Barbara Brabec is the editor of the *National Home Business Report,* a national home business newsletter since 1981. (See the magazine and newsletter chapter.) So she really knows what she's talking about in her books: *Homemade Money: The Definitive Guide to Success in a Home Business.* This highly successful book is in its third edition, and is very popular. It is literally three books in one. First there's an A-Z crash course in business basics. Then there's a comprehensive marketing section, including many trade secrets and advice from professionals in the field. The third section is a 500 listing resource chapter. There's even more: a computer overview; an overview of the home business industry, and stress management tips.Highly recommended, contains information that will help new or experienced home businesses. 325 pages, $18.95 postpaid.

A companion book to *Homemade Money* is Barbara Brabec's *HELP for Your Homebased Business.* This book is designed for people who have started a home business, but it has not yet fully blossomed. Many readers of her first book have contributed advice for this book, and there's also some of the best material from her newsletter.128 pages, $13.45 postpaid.

Creative Cash: Making Money with Your Crafts, Needlework, Designs & Know-How continues the fine tradition of knowledgeable home business advice by showing how to set up a craft business, how to buy supplies wholesale, how to success at crafts sales, how to get into mail order, and even how to profit through teaching your skills to others! 208 pages, $13.95 postpaid. A companion book to this is *A Treasury Trove of Crafts Marketing Success Secrets.* This book gives you the advice that Barbara has received though letters from crafts people all across the country. There's information on what shop owners expect from a craft seller, how to use cooperative craft shops to make a profit, how to work with sales reps, and more. 104 pages, $11.45 postpaid.

Bell Springs Publishing, Administrative Offices Address: PO Box 640, Bell Springs Road, Laytonville CA 95454. (707) 984-6746. Orders Address & Phone: PO Box 870, Occidental CA 95465. (707) 578-1135. This company publishes several good books for home businesses. One is *Small Time Operator: How to Start Your Own Business, Keep Your Books, Pay*

Your Taxes, & Stay Out of Trouble by Bernard Kamoroff. This book has been a consistently good seller because it is an essential guide for any home-based business. It explains various legal and financial aspects of business that everyone should know. It has been so popular that the company has produced a sequel, which you can read about in their catalog. 192 pages, $12.95.

Another good book is *We Own It: Starting and Managing Coops, Collectives, & Employee-Owned Ventures* by Peter Jan Honigsberg, Bernard Kamoroff & Jim Beatty. Coops are excellent outlets for products from home businesses, and this book explains the legal, financial, managerial procedures for all sorts of coops. This book is clear, concise, and gives lots of examples. Hardcover, 164 pages, $16.95.

This company also distributes home business books for other publishers. For instance, they carry McGraw Hill's *Getting Into Mail Order* by Julian Simon, $14.95. Send for Bell Publishing's free catalog (catalog available through order address) and see their list of home business books.

Betterway Publications, PO Box 219, Crozet VA 22932. (804) 823-5661. Publishers of *Homemade Money* by Barbara Brabec, an excellent book on how to earn money from home. Barbara Brabec is the editor of the *National Home Business Report,* a national home business newsletter since 1981. (See the magazine and newsletter chapter.) So she really knows what she's talking about in her books. This highly successful book is in its third edition, and is very popular. It is literally three books in one. First there's an A-Z crash course in business basics. Then there's a comprehensive marketing section, including many trade secrets and advice from professionals in the field. The third section is a 500 listing resource chapter. There's even more: a computer overview; an overview of the home business industry, and stress management tips.325 pages, $18.95 postpaid.

Homemade Money
by Barbara Brabec
Betterway Publications

Other home business books available are: *Stay Home and Mind Your Own Business: How to Manager Your Time, Space, Personal Obligations, Money, Business and Yourself While*

Stay Home & Mind Your Own Business
by Jo Frohbieter-Mueller
Betterway Publications

Working at Home by Jo Frohbieter-Mueller. A home business person must perform a delicate balancing act: juggling business time, personal time, and socializing time. At person working at home will benefit from this look at relationships (family, friends, relatives, community) and how they affect the business at home. This book also looks at business itself: everything from choosing an appropriate product to bookkeeping to collection policies. 280 pages, $9.95.

The Small Business Information Source Book by Adrian A. Paradis. A guidebook to finding information on numerous subjects of interest to small businesses. For instance, if you need to find information on alcoholism, it's listed alphabetically between "Affirmative Action" and "American Dates and Facts". The "Alcoholism" listing gives general information and addresses of the National Council of Alcoholism, Al-Anon Family Group Headquarters, and Alcoholics Anonymous World Headquarters. The first part of the book is listings such as these on various subjects. A few more subjects included are: "Fringe Benefits," "Illegal Aliens," "Postal Rates and Service," "Social Security," and "State Labor Departments." The second part of the book lists organizations of interest to small businesses, also listed alphabetically by subject matters. For instance, under the heading of "Aluminum" there's the Aluminum Association with its address. Under "Paper" is the listing American Paper Institute with its address. There's headings for such things as farming, engineering, optics, railroads, securities regulations, wool, etc. 136 pages, $7.95.

Homegrown Computer Profits: A Comprehensive Guide for the Home Business Entrepreneur by Marsha Kee Chandler. Since the computer revolution is a major reason that so many home businesses are now in existence, this book is an obvious plus. It is a user-friendly (easy to read and use) guide for home businesses, whether or not they are already using a computer. It tells how the computer will help make their business more efficient, and then goes on to explain what type of computer and software will meet their needs. 160 pages, $9.95.

Cleaning Up for a Living: Everything You Need to Know to Become a

Successful Building Service Contractor by Don Aslett & Mark Browning.One business that a person can start at home is a professional cleaning service. This book is an informative (and humorous!) explanation of how to start this type of business. Includes forms, charts, and equipment lists, as well as chapters on advertising, marketing, pricing, and dealing with the competition. 204 pages, $12.95.

B. Klein Publications, PO Box 8503, Coral Springs FL 33065. (305) 752-1708. This company publishes a directory called *Directory of Mailing List Houses*. Provides the names of more than 1400 mailing list specialists including brokers, compilers, management companies, cooperative mailers, card deck mailers, and more. Arranged geographically and fully indexed. 240 pages. $65. Also offers *Mail Order Business Directory,* with over 10,000 of the most active mail order and catalog houses in the US. Listed geographically. 450 pages, $75. A new title is *Mail Order Product Guide,* listing more than 1400 US and foreign manufacturers. 240 pages, $65. These three books are also offered in mailing list format. See mailing list chapter.

Other books offered by this company that might be of interest to home businesses are: *Computer Entrepreneur,* that shows how to make money in your spare time using a personal computer. Explains how to find the business best suited to your talents and background. 900 pages, $50. *How Mail Order Fortunes are Made,* describes the operation and organization of successful mail order businesses. 352 pages, $25. *Mail Order Legal Manual,* to help you keep up with the increasing state and federal regulations concerning mail order. 400 pages, $55. *Making $500,000 a Year in Mail Order,* where an expert shows you exactly what steps to make to profit from mail order. 200 pages, $25.

National Directory of Postcard Deck Media, the information you need to plan your card deck advertising program. 250 pages, $65. *Directory of High Discount Merchandise Sources,* lists more than 1200 sources of products offered at high discounts. 116 pages, $35. *Franchise Manual,* lists 2500 franchisors, distributors, licensors and franchise consultants. 200 pages, $30.

Add $3 shipping for first book, $1 each additional book. This company also offers distributorships for selling their books. Check distributor chapter.

Bluestocking Press/ Educational Sprectrums, PO Box 1014, Placerville CA 95667. (916) 621-1123. This company specializes in informative books. One of their valuable titles for home business is *Whatever Happened to Penny Candy?* by Richard J. Maybury. This is a fast, clear and fun explanation of the economics you need for success in your career, business and investments. In other words, read this and you will understand a lot more about money and how it works in our economy. It's so well-written that it has a fine endorsement from William E. Simon, former US Secretary of the Treasury, "This is a delightful, very informative and easy-to-read primer in free market economics for young adults, written with a great deal of charm.....It is must reading for anyone who wishes to understand the basics of our free enterprise system." $4.95.

This company has a good catalog of highly recommended books. In the section of the catalog marked "Work Options for Parents and Children" there are three very good home business books: *Work-at-Home Sourcebook* by Lynnie Arden (editor and publisher of *Worksteader News*), which lists over 1,000 companies that have work-at-home arrangements. $12.95. *Growing a Business/ Raising a Family* edited by Jan and Charlie Fletcher (editors and publishers of the *Home Business Advisor* newsletter), that contains ideas and inspirations for the work-at-home parent. Fun reading, $8.50. *Homemade Money* by Barbara Brabec (editor of the *National Home Business Report*), an excellent book on how to earn money from home. This highly successful book is in its third edition, and is very popular. It is literally three books in one. First there's an A-Z crash course in business basics. Then there's a comprehensive marketing section, including many trade secrets and advice from professionals in the field. The third section is a 500 listing resource chapter. There's even more: a computer overview; an overview of the home business industry, and stress management tips.325 pages, $18.95 postpaid.

Camera Ventures, Photomoney Division, PO Box 771, Lamar CO 81052. Numerous publications priced from $1 to $25 on how to sell your photos, making money with a camera, etc. All guaranteed. Send for list. Also has a mailing list of over 30,000 active photographers and camera enthusiasts, most of whom are interested in home business opportunities.

Computer Information Ltd., PO Box 25130, 7040 Hawaii Kai Drive, Honolulu HI 96825. 1-800-528-3665. FAX (808) 395-1045. Catalog full of books to teach you how to earn money with your computer. *The Sampler* is a book of brief outlines of all 100 personal computer businesses, including a self-test to determine which one is best for you. 110 pages, $20. *The Big 10* book describes the ten most popular personal computer businesses that have consistently been proven money makers. $25. *Source Manual* tells where to find software, hardware, manuals and reports for personal computer businesses. $20. More titles available in this catalog. If you're interested in personal computer business, see chapter on organizations as well.

Contemporary Books, Inc., 3250 South Western Avenue, Chicago IL 60608. (312) 782-9181. *How to Start a Professional Photography Business* by Ted Schwarz. A complete guide to making photography pay, from assembling a portfolio to advertising to public relations, to getting along with clients. There's a lot of information about specialty photography: wedding photography, public relations photography, architectural photography, fashion photography, baby photography, advertising photography, and more. 276 pages, $11.95.

How to Be a Freelance Photography by Ted Schwarz. The author lets you know that freelance photography really is possible for you, regardless of what camera you own. You really can break into this exciting field. First he lets you know what the market is for photos, then he tells you how to sell them. He explores several market areas: book market, overseas market, and freelance photo stories. 152 pages, $9.95.

Darian Books, PO Box 3091, Glendale AZ 85311. (602) 931-3788. *How to Earn $15 to $50 an Hour & More With a Pickup Truck or Van* by Don Lilly. Step-by-step guide to equipment, legal matters, advertising, hiring help, record-keeping, and everything you need for using a vehicle to earn money. Lists numerous ideas for earning money with just a vehicle plus a few simple tools. These ideas are applicable anywhere, are simple, yet realistic. The author gives clear-cut examples from his own experience and throws in excellent advice that will save a person many hours of frustration. 128 pages. $14.20 postpaid.

Darian Books distributes home business books for other publishers. One interesting titles is *Everything You Need to Know to Start a House Cleaning Service,* that gives detailed information about how to price a job for profit, how to sell your services, finding and keeping employees, crew procedures, cleaning techniques and products. $16.20 postpaid. Also distributes *Flea Market Handbook* that shows how you can, without much money, set up a business at a nearby flea market and make your collection grow into a small fortune. All tricks of the trade are covered: how to deal with cranky customers, how to buy from auctions, how to turn a haggler into a buyer, how to keep necessary records, and how to build an expanding business. 156 pages, $11.20 postpaid.

Send for the brochure "Darian Bookshelf" to keep updated on current titles that they distribute.

Dennis Weaver, 1010 Cantey, Fort Worth TX 76104. *How to Start Your First Business* by J. Edward Bronson. Reveals eight businesses specifically taylored for the beginning businessman that require no special education, can be started in the home, can be started part-time, can be run by one person, require little or no investment, and are simple to get started. $15. *How to Make Money in Your Own Mailorder Business* by Jack Erbe. $15. And *101 Easy Businesses You Can Start Now—Even If You're Just About Flat Broke* by Eric Getch. Describes 101 honest, down-home businesses that can be started with little or no cash, can be started immediately, and will actually generate profits! $15.

Doubleday & Company, 245 Park Ave., New York NY 10167. (212) 953-4561. *Nine Easy Steps to Turn Rummage into Cash: Rummage, Tag & Garage Sales for Profit & Fun!* by Irma & P.A. Pohl. Fun, easy book that's well organized and packed with lots of information about how to clean out your closets, garages, and storage sheds, and have a successful garage sale. Topics covered in the book are types of sales, location, time selection, managing inventory, advertising, pricing, neighborhood sales, flea markets, and rummage sales as a part-time business. 128 pages. $4.95.

Eden Press, 5201 Nagel Drive., Cheektowaga NY 14225. In Canada: 5201 Dufferin Rd., Downsview, Ontario M3H 5T8. *How to Make Big Money at Home* by Ronald J. Cooke. Contains case histories of business successes and then 55 specific ideas for home-based businesses. Some of these are quite original, such as "Prints from Europe," "Be a Garage-Sale Manager," and "Land for Quick Cash Crops." Also some advice on setting up the business, such as "How Much Capital Do You Need?" "Cutting Start-Up Costs," and "What About a Partnership?" 116 pages, $9.95.

Fair Oaks Publishing Company, 941 Populus Place, Sunnyvale CA 94086. (408) 732-1078. Publishes a very popular and attractive book: *Starting a Mini-Business: A Guidebook for Seniors* (Revised Edition) by Nancy Olsen. Although specifically designed for those age 55 and over who are seeking to supplement retirement income, this book has appeal for anyone interested in starting a part-time, low-risk home business. It's a step-by-step guide that starts at the beginning, helps generate ideas, helps the novice business person get established, teaches how to keep records and get marketing started, and other useful advice. A special appendix has written exercises designed to help the person get started, such as "Is a Mini-Business the Right Thing for Me?" and "Defining My Business Idea." $8.95.

Fleming LTD, PO Box 1738, Davis CA 95617-1738. Publishers of *Electronic Cottage Handbook #1 and #2*. #1 has 20 building blocks for your home business, explains marketing and what equipment you will need for using your computer in a home business, and a resource guide. $10 postpaid. #2 tells about the top home computer businesses. $7 postpaid. Also publishes *How to Start a Word Processing Business* which profiles word processing entrepreneurs, gives a resource guide, and tells how to get started. $6 postpaid.

The Front Room, 63 Starmond Ave., Clifton NY 07013. (Mail address: PO

Box 1541, Clifton NJ 07501-1541.) (201) 773-4215. Publishes books and booklets that teach how to market crafts. Their catalog also offers titles from other publishers and is very helpful to a home-based business.

Some of the titles found in the catalog are: "How to Market Your Handcrafts to Shops," 22 pages, $5. "How to Purchase Supplies Wholesale," 14 pages, $3.50. "Directory of Craft Shops," updated yearly, 38 pages, $6.95. "Directory of Wholesale Reps for Artisans," $6.50. "Marketing Crafts Through Home Parties," $6.95. "Selling to Catalog Houses," $12.95. "The Law (in Plain English) for Craftspeople," 143 pages, $9.50. And one of their popular titles is "Pattern Designer Directory," $12.95 ppd.

Send for their Learning Extension Catalog for a complete list of books and booklets.

The Globe Pequot Press, Inc, Old Chester Road, Chester CT 06412. (203) 526-9571. *How to Open and Operate a Bed & Breakfast Home* by Jan Stankus. This authoritative handbook helps you decide if you would make a good B&B host; what it takes to run a successful B&B, how to price the rooms, how to list with a reservation service, how to publicize your B&B, how to screen your guests, plus much more information. Special appendices list reservation service organizations and state/local tourist offices. Wonderful reviews have been written about this book, including those form Better Homes & Gardens, Changing Times, Country Living, Homebased Entrepreneur Newsletter, and other publications. 290 pages, $11.95.

Great Stuff Studios, 6617 Portsmouth Lane, Raleigh NC 27615. (919) 846-2961. The main service of this home-based business is designing logos, offering marketing advice, writing brochures and other publicity items for home-based businesses. However, they also offer twelve reports of interest to those investigating the possibility of starting a home business. They offer a brochure listing these reports for a long SASE. Ask for their "Publications for Small and Home-Based Businesses." Topics of these reports include: "How to create a brochure even if you have no money and no art skills," $3; "Planning for a better newsletter," $2; "But what can I do at home?" $2; "Selling calligraphy," $1.50.

Henry-Madison Research, Box 1281-HB, Orangevale CA 95662. (916) 624-2766. FAX (916) 632-2501. Publisher of special reports to help business people and investors. One title is *How You Can Find Good Financial Advice* by Richard J. Maybury, business and economics analyst. Provides a checklist of 13 important questions you should ask before making investments, how to avoid pitfalls and rip-offs, and recommended investments.36 pages, $14.95.

Also available is *Whatever Happened to Penny Candy?* by Richard J.

Maybury. This is a fast, clear and fun explanation of the economics you need for success in your career, business and investments. In other words, read this and you will understand a lot more about money and how it works in our economy. It's so well-written that it has a fine endorsement from William E. Simon, former US Secretary of the Treasury, "This is a delightful, very informative and easy-to-read primer in free market economics for young adults, written with a great deal of charm.....It is must reading for anyone who wishes to understand the basics of our free enterprise system." $4.95. Add $2 for shipping each book.

Jeffrey Lant Associates, 50 Follen St, Ste 507, Cambridge MA 02138. Jeffrey Lant's Sure-Fire Business Success Catalog contains numerous books and reports to help the business person. Many of these are very applicable to home businesses. His most famous product is called *The Unabashed Self-Promoter's Guide.* This is probably the most important publicity book ever written. $34. Another useful title is *The Consultant's Kit: Establishing and Operating Your Successful Consulting Business,* especially if you plan to be any type of consultant. $34.

There are several marketing titles, self-publishing titles, and mail-order money-making titles. Also *How to Start Your Own Business on a Shoestring and Make Up To $500,000 a Year* by Tyler Hicks. Lists over 1,000 businesses you can run from your home. $12.95. Barbara Brabec's *Homemade Money* is available, $19.95.

Work-at-Home Sourcebook
by Lynnie Arden
Live Oak Publications

Live Oak Publications, PO Box 2193, Boulder CO 80306. (street address: 1515 23rd St, Boulder CO 80302). *The Work-at-Home Sourcebook* by Lynnie Arden is one of the books everyone considering a home business must have! There is so much information contained in this book that it will always be a valuable resource. This book tells about companies that routinely use home-based workers as part of their work force. The chapters tell about real opportunities in art, crafts, telecommuting, computer, office support, sales, and much more. Each company listed has its address, the positions it offers to home-based workers, its requirements, and other information, such as pay scale. The book is well organized, and even has the companies indexed by alphabet and geographical regions. There's a special index for companies that offer special home-based programs for the handicapped worker.219 pages, $14.95 postpaid. Free brochure on request.

Mothers' Home Business Network, PO Box 423, East Meadow NY 11554. This is an organization for mothers with home-based businesses. They publish a booklet called *Mothering and Managing a Typing Service at Home*. Helpful hints on how to manage both the kids and a home business, specifically a typing service. 15 pages, $5 postpaid.

NextStep Publications, 6340 34th SW, Seattle WA 98126-3148. (206) 938-2290. Publishes a very extraordinary book called *Growing a Business/ Raising a Family: Ideas and Inspiration for the Work-at-Home Parent* edited by Jan and Charlie Fletcher. These editors have established a highly successful publishing company that not only publishes this book, but also the Home Business Advisor newsletter (see chapter on magazines and newsletters). This book is a collection of essays based on home-based parents' first-hand experiences in growing a business while raising a family. Some of the articles are: "Starting a Home Business: The Emotional Journey," "Whole-Life

Growing a Business/ Raising a Family
Jan & Charlie Fletcher
NextStep Publications

Integration," "Portrait of a Family Business," and "Making Time for Work and Family." One of the essays has been reprinted in this book with their permission, "Twenty Questions to Ask Yourself." The articles have been prepared by some of the writers who contribute to their newsletter, and provide practical advice while continuing to inspire the work-at-home parent. It's great reading. Highly recommended. 121 pages plus some home business ads, $9.95 postpaid.

P & P Publications, PO Box 725295, Atlanta GA 30339. (404) 952-8734. *The Complete Guide to Homemade Income* by Paul Purcell. Lists 187 ideas for home businesses. Examples:

PVC pipe furniture, hoodcleaning service, new mother's maid, baby sitter broker, shuttle service, shopping cart collector, and much more. Many of these services described are unique, but quite realistic if applied in a professional manner. $7.95.

Para Publishing, PO Box 4232, Santa Barbara CA 93140-4232. (805) 968-7277. For orders, call 1-800-PARAPUB. This company sells everything you need to become a publisher. Thousands of publishers around the world began by reading Dan Poynter's book *The Self-Publishing Manual.* The book has been revised and reprinted many times, making it one of the best-selling books on publishing. The information is clear, easy to follow, complete, and precise. His advice really does help a person become a real publisher, from concept to book to marketing. 1989 edition, 420 pages, $19.95.

Another excellent title for people thinking about publishing is *Is There a Book Inside You?* by Dan Poynter and Mindy Bingham. It teaches you to author a book whether or not you have the time or ability to be a good writer. Amazing information! 240 pages, $9.95.

Publishing Short-Run Books introduces you to the new techniques and machinery that enables you to by-pass costly graphic artists and commercial printers. Perfect for producing inexpensive newsletters, fliers, and brochures. 5th edition, 1989, 144 pages, $5.95. For a complete list of their titles, ask for "Book Publishing Resources from Dan Poynter". All products carry a personal guarantee from Dan Poynter.

In addition to their own books, this company carries a line of selected titles on publishing by other authors. Ask for "Author/ Publisher Bookshelf". Also-Dan Poynter opens his home overlooking the Pacific just five times a year for detailed seminars on publishing. This is truly a magnificent offer, because Mr. Poynter knows the business inside and out.

Other publishing helps available are reports on subjects such as brochure printing, buying book printing, co-op book promotion, beyond remainders, and others. You can also purchase mailing lists for marketing books, such as book reviewers, book wholesalers, distributors, book clubs, and more. Dan prepares a newsletter called "Publishing Poynters" which is filled with tips and ideas and is mailed free to publishers around the world.

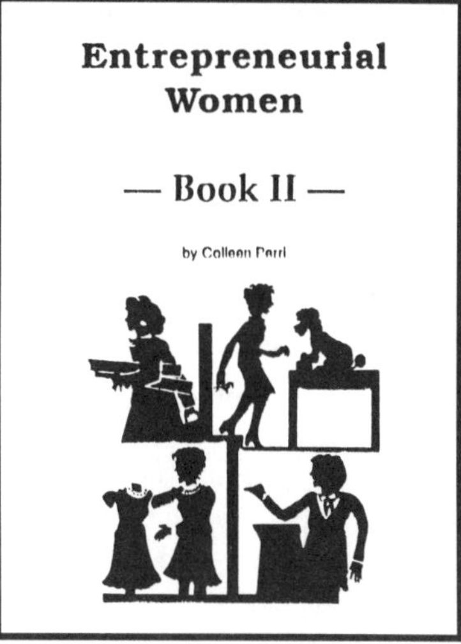

Entrepreneurial Women
by Colleen Perri
Possibilities Publishing

Possibilities Publishing, Colleen A. Perri, 2103 33rd St., Kenosha WI 53140. (414) 652-6516. Publishes *Entrepreneurial Women* by Colleen Perri, subtitled: "23 Kenosha women share their success stories." This book profiles 23 women and their businesses; some are home-based and some are located in stores. Some of the businesses started in the home and then expanded into stores. For instance, Gayle Chiodo sells Indian arts and crafts from her home and through specialty shows. She tells how she started as a hobbyist and then developed into a dealer.

Some of the other home-based women are involved in country crafts, cake baking, antiques, laundry service, and home day care. The advantage of a book like this is that these are real people who have really succeeded at these businesses, so their tips are exceptionally helpful.

There is a sequel to this successful book called *Entrepreneurial Women, Book II* by Colleen Perri. This book has 21 more success stories. 142 pages, $12.95.

This company offers other materials useful to home businesses, such as the report "How to Become a Hometown Author," $5; "Self-Publishing," $5.

Prentice Hall, 1 Gulf+ Western Plaza, New York NY 10023. (212) 373-8500. FAX (212) 373-8292. *The Small Business Handbook* by Irving Burstiner. This is a comprehensive guide to starting and running your own business. Includes: finding the right business for you, targeting customers, getting financing, choosing a location, hiring employees, marketing products, pricing procedures, advertising, distribution, and planning processes. This is an essential guide to avoiding the common start-up problems and turning a business into a lasting success. 356 pages, $16.95.

Profit Ideas, 254 E Grand Ave, Escondido CA 92025. (619) 432-8375. Several well-known success and money books available. *Stay Home & Make Money* (formerly titled *A Treasury of Home Business Opportunities*) by Russ von Hoelscher. Newly revised edition. Current information on ideas for types of home businesses (including special services that are now extremely in demand) and how to start, plus lots of extra valuable information. This revised edition also has a special section on big profit opportunities in advertising, writing, direct marketing, and mail order. This man is an expert in this field, and his advice is worth listening to. He has made a successful business from publishing and now has worldwide distributors. 310 pages, $12.95.

Selling Information by Mail by Russ von Hoelscher. He teaches how to find saleable information products, how to self-publish the material, how to successfully use classified and display advertising to make a profit selling this information, and how to obtain free advertising and publicity. 225 pages, $12.95.

How to Achieve Total Success by Russ von Hoelscher. There are over 100,000 copies of this book in print worldwide. This book is an explanation about how to use your "mind dynamic" to achieve your goals. There's development of such topics as "Scientific Affirmations," Creative Affirmations," and the "Success Covenant." It's a positive-life book. 442 pages. $12.95.

Other good titles from this company are: *Real Estate Wealth-Building Opportunities; Making Money for Yourself; & Secrets of the Millionaires*. Each book is $12.95; add $1 for shipping of each book ordered. You can start a home business by being a distributor of these books. See chapter on distributorships in this book.

Roundtable Publishing, 933 Pico Blvd, Santa Monica CA 90405. (213) 450-9777. *The Business of Family Day Care* by Helen McCrorey and Dolores McCrorey, 104 pages, $12.95. This book helps solve problems specifically found in home day care, such as: the legal issues concerning family day care; how to screen the people you will be providing care for; how to develop a good contract for this particular business; how to deal with difficult situations such as delinquent payments and the problem child or the problem parent; and the basics of day care. It's easy to read and very informative for this type of business.

San Juan Naturals, PO Box 642, Friday Harbor WA 98250. (206) 378-2648. *Profits From Your Backyard Herb Garden* by Lee Sturdivant. Earn $50 to $250 weekly from a small area in your spare time. Complete details on marketing, growing, and packaging culinary herbs. Satisfaction guaranteed. 120 pages, $11.95 postpaid.

Storey Communications, Schoolhouse Road, Pownal VT 05261. (802) 823-5811. Orders 1-800-441-5700. *Cash from Square Foot Gardening* by Mel Bartholomew. The author of this book is the star of his own PBS television series. In this book he explains his square-foot gardening method, a simple and effective way to not only provide fresh produce for your own family, but also to develop bountiful cash crops from the tiniest growing space. He tells you how to grow the vegetables that will bring the highest prices, and how to sell at a handsome profit. 256 pages, $9.95.

Cash from Square Foot Gardening
by Mel Bartholomew
Storey Communications

Sunshine Sales, 211 W 3rd St., PO Box 931, Byron IL 61010-0931. (815) 234-5648. Sells success and money books by mail. Send for brochures.

TAB Books, Blue Ridge Summit PA 17294-0850. (717) 794-2191. Liberty, a division of TAB Books, publishes *Becoming Self-Employed: First-Hand Advice From Those Who Have Done It!* by Susan Elliott. This book profiles twenty cases of successful entrepreneurs. Reveals the secrets of success for financing, marketing, productivity, and more. Types of businesses discussed include: art gallery, country inn, restaurant, antique dealer, book store, performer, illustrator, winemaker, consultant, etc. Many of these are home-based businesses and the ideas presented blend with this type of atmosphere. $7.95.

A new title is one they distribute for Liberty House called Home-Based Mail Order: A Success Guide for Entrepreneurs by William J. Bond. Mr. Bond brings over 25 years of mail order experience to this book, providing readers with realistic advice and solid plans for succeeding in home mail order—while incurring minimal financial risk. Paper, 224 pages, $14.95.

TAB Books is a distributor as well as a publisher, and their catalog contains many informative books for home-based businesses. For instance:

WORKING TOGETHER: Entrepreneurial Couples by Frank & Sharah Barnett

Ten Speed Press

Start & Run a Profitable Consulting Business, $12.95; *Start & Run a Profitable Craft Business*, $10.95; *The #1 Home Business Book*, $7.95, *Becoming Self-Employed: How to Create an Independent Livelihood,* 160 pages, $7.95. Send for books price list.

Ten Speed Press/ Celestial Arts, PO Box 7123, Berkeley CA 94707. (415) 845-8414. Orders: 1-800-841-BOOK. FAX (415) 524-1052. This company became famous for their book *What Color is Your Parachute?*, a job-hunter's manual, which is in the nth printing and revised for 1989. But they have a full catalog of great books, including some for the home business.

How to be an Importer and Pay for Your World Travel by Mary Green and Stanley Gillmar. The author's backgrounds pretty much explain why this book is so useful: Mary is the founder of a successful import company in San Francisco and Stanley is an attorney experienced in import/export and international law. So the book covers a great many details, not only about where to go, what to buy, and how to deal with customs, but also has appendices containing US Customs brochures, forms for letters of credit, a glossary for import terms, and a list of annual foreign trade fairs. 192 pages, $6.95.

Working Together: Entrepreneurial Couples, by Frank & Sharan Barnett. Since this book is written by a couple who have worked together successfully (their own advertising agency), it can also successfully look at this type of lifestyle. Couples who work together have learned that together they can realize their goals. The book explores the limitless potentials for work and leisure for couple who have decided that "together" means in all facets of life. The book even coins a word, "copreneur", and shows how to end separate lives. This is truly a pattern for living for the future. 256 pages. $9.95.

Making $70,000+ a Year as a Self-Employed Manufacturer's Representative by Leigh and Sureleigh Silliphant. Many companies hire independent sales reps, and this book shows how to break into that market. This can be one way a person develops a business based from home. A successful manufacturer's rep can also travel and earn at the same time. 224 pages, $9.95.

That's a Great Idea by Tony Husch & Linda Foust. A guide for how to get, evaluate, protect, develop, and sell new product ideas. Includes a lengthy resource guide for publications, associations, newsletters, small business development centers, government agencies and federal patent libraries, along with sample forms for confidentiality and licensing agreements. This book has received many favorable reviews from knowledgeable experts such as *The Home Business Advocate, Marketing News* (of American Marketing Association), *The Idealog, Journal of the Brain Exchange, Akron Business Reporter, Technology Management News, Publishers Weekly, Information Marketing, National Home Business Report, The Lightbulb* (Inventors Workshop International Education Foundation), and many more! 256 pages, $9.95.

Universal Developments Publishing, PO Box 5253, Orange CA 92667. *How to Cash in On Your Bright Ideas* by George G. Siposs, MBA. This book shows step-by-step how to turn an idea into a product and then how to make a business out of it. Chapters cover: low cost ways to protect ideas; developing the prototype; low volume manufacturing with no overhead; gaining free publicity; how to get royalty payments, and more. 260 pages. $10 postpaid.

Valerie Fisher, 6836 Duckling Way, Sacramento CA 95842. (916) 332-8993. Several booklets are available to help handcrafters earn profits. Send SASE for information, request "Crafting Your Way to Profits" brochure. Booklets include, "Crafts for Profit", $6; "Craft Fairs", $1; "Wholesale Sales Reps", $1; "Buying Wholesale", $3; "Sources", $5; "Catalog Layouts for Do-It-Yourselfers", $3.25; "Finding and Dealing with Sales Reps", $1.75; "Crafting Home Parties", $5. All prices postpaid.

William Morrow and Company, Inc., 105 Madison Ave., New York NY 10016. (212) 889-3050. *How to Create Your Own Fad and Make a Million Dollars* by Ken Hakuta. Lots of people dream of becoming millionaires by coming up with their own Pet Rock, Mood Ring, or other fad that will sell explosively and make millions of dollars. But how do you get the right product, market it successfully and quickly before someone else steps in and mimics your product, finance your product, get exclusive rights, get the right distributors, and even turn a fad into a classic? This book can tell you how, by someone who's done it. Even though he has a MBA degree, he realized that selling his life for $75,000 a year wasn't for him. He started a successful fad, and can tell you how. 226. pages, $12.95.

Yowdabar Inc., 395 Mt. Rd., West Monroe LA 71291. (318) 397-1942.

Start and Operate a Successful Janitorial Business Using Subcontractors. The book contains all the know-how necessary to start and operate a successful janitorial business, including what types of chemicals and supplies to use, the forms you need, how to find clients, how to negotiate a contract, and how to generate profits. There's a whole special section of the book devoted to cleaning operations—best ways to clean glass; deodorizing effectively, carpet cleaning, vacuuming techniques, floor sealing and varnish, etc. 51 pages, $18.

EDITOR'S LIST OF RECOMMENDED BOOKS
Her favorites are marked with ***

Word Processing Profits at Home, Aames-Allen Publishing.

****Homemade Money,* Betterway Publications. (Also distributed by Bluestocking Press/Educational Spectrums, Barbara Brabec Productions, & Jeffrey Lant Associates.)

Stay Home and Mind Your Own Business, Betterway Publications.

Whatever Happened to Penny Candy? Bluestocking Press/Educational Spectrums & Henry-Madison Research.

****Self-Publishing Manual,* Para Publishing.

****Work at Home Sourcebook,* Live Oak Publications (Also distributed by Bluestocking Press/Educational Spectrums.

****Growing a Business/ Raising a Family,* NextStep Publications. (Also distributed by Bluestocking Press/ Educational Spectrums.)

How to Earn $15 to $50 an Hour & More With a Pickup Truck or Van , Darian Books.

Starting a Mini-Business: A Guidebook for Seniors, Fair Oaks Publishing.

The Unabashed Self-Promoters Guide, Jeffrey Lant Associates.

Entrepreneurial Women, Possibilities Publishing.

Stay Home & Make Money, (formerly titled A Treasury of Home Business Opportunities) Profit Ideas.

****Working Together: Entrepreneurial Couples,* Ten Speed Press.

Alphabetical listing of books in this chapter

Publisher's name follows title for easy cross-reference

America's New Breed of Entrepreneurs: Their Marketing Strategies, Techniques & Successes (Acropolis Books Ltd)

A Treasury Trove of Crafts Marketing Success Secrets (Barbara Brabec Productions)

Becoming Self-Employed: First-Hand Advice From Those Who Have Done It (TAB Books)

Becoming Self-Employed: How to Create an Independent Livelihood (TAB Books)

The Business of Family Day Care (Roundtable Publishing)

Cash From Square Foot Gardening (Storey Communications)

Cleaning Up For a Living: Everything You Need to Know to Become a Successful Building Service Contractor (Betterway Publications)

The Complete Guide to Homemade Income (P & P Publications)

Computer Entrepreneur (B. Klein Publications)

The Consultant's Kit: Establishing and Operating Your Successful Consulting Business (Jeffrey Lant Associates)

Creative Cash: Making Money with Your Crafts, Needlework, Designs & Know-How (Barbara Brabec Productions)

Directory of Crafts Shops (The Front Room)

Directory of Mailing List Houses (B. Klein Publications)

Directory of Wholesale Reps for Artisans (The Front Room)

Electronic Cottage Handbook (Fleming LTD)

Entrepreneurial Women (Possibilities Publishing)

Entrepreneurial Women, Book II (Possibilities Publishing)

Everything You Need to Know to Start a House Cleaning Service (Darian Books)

Flea Market Handbook (Darian Books)

Growing a Business/ Raising a Family (NextStep Publications)

Help for Your Homebased Business (Barbara Brabec Productions)

Homebased Mail Order: A Success Guide for Entrepreneurs (TAB Books)

Homegrown Computer Profits:A Comprehensive Guide for the Home Business Entrepreneur (Betterway Publications)

Homemade Money (Betterway Publications)

How Mail Order Fortunes are Made (B. Klein Publications)

How to Achieve Total Success (Profit Ideas)

How to Be a Freelance Photographer (Contemporary Books Inc.)

How to Be an Importer and Pay for Your World Travel (Ten Speed Press/ Celestial Arts)

How to Cash in On Your Bright Ideas (Universal Developments)

How to Create Your Own Fad and Make a Million Dollars (William Morrow & Company)

How to Earn $15 to $50 an Hour & More With a Pickup Truck or Van (Darian Books)

How to Make Big Money at Home (Eden Press)

How to Make Money in Your Own Mailorder Business (Dennis Weaver)

How to Market Your Handcrafts to Shops (The Front Room)

How to Open and Operate a Bed & Breakfast Home (Globe Pequot Press Inc)

How to Purchase Supplies Wholesale (The Front Room)

How to Start and Run a Successful Home Typing Business (Aames-Allen Publishing)

How to Start a Professional Photography Business (Contemporary Books, Inc.)

How to Start a Word Processing Business (Fleming LTD)

How to Start Your First Business (Dennis Weaver)

How to Start Your Own Business on a Shoestring and Make up to $500,000 a Year (Jeffrey Lant Associates)

How You Can Find Good Financial Advice (Henry-Madison Research)

Image Consulting: The New Career (Acropolis Books Ltd)

Is There a Book Inside You? (Para Publishing)

The Law—in Plain English—for Craftspeople (The Front Room)

Mail Order Business Directory (B. Klein Publications)

Mail Order Legal Manual (B. Klein Publications)

Making $70,000+ a Year as a Self-Employed Manufacturer's Represenative (Ten Speed Press/ Celestial Arts)

Making $500,000 a Year in Mail Order (B. Klein Publications)

Making It On Your Own (Acropolis Books Ltd)

Making Money for Yourself (Profit Ideas)

Marketing Crafts Through Home Parties (The Front Room)

Mothering and Managing a Typing Service at Home (Mothers' Home Business Network)

National Directory of Postcard Deck Media (B. Klein Publications)

Nine Easy Steps to Turn Rummage into Cash (Doubleday & Company)

Pattern Designer Directory (The Front Room)

Profits From Your Backyard Herb Garden (San Juan Naturals)

Publications for Small and Home-Based Businesses (Great Stuff Studios)

Publishing Short-Run Books (Para Publishing)

Real Estate Wealth-Building Opportunities (Profit Ideas)

Secrets of the Millionaires (Profit Ideas)

Self-Publishing Manual (Para Publishing)

Selling Information by Mail (Profit Ideas)

Selling to Catalog Houses (The Front Room)

Sell Like a Pro (Acropolis Books Ltd)

The Small Business Handbook (Prentice Hall)

The Small Business Information Source Book (Betterway Publications)

Small Time Operator (Bell Springs Publishing)

Start & Operate a Successful Janitorial Service Using Subcontractors (Yowdabar Inc)

Start & Run a Profitable Consulting Business (TAB Books)

Start & Run a Profitable Craft Business (TAB Books)

Starting a Mini-Business: A Guidebook for Seniors (Fair Oaks Publishing)

Stay Home & Make Money (Profit Ideas)

Stay Home & Mind Your Own Business (Betterway Publications)

That's a Great Idea (Ten Speed Press/ Celestial Arts)

The #1 Home Business Books (TAB Books)

The Unabashed Self-Promoter's Guide (Jeffrey Lant Associates)

We Own It: Starting and Managing Coops, Collectives & Employee-Owned Ventures (Bell Springs Publishing)

Whatever Happened to Penny Candy (Henry-Madison Research & Bluestocking Press/ Educational Spectrums)

Word Processing Profits at Home (Aames-Allen Publishing)

Work-at-Home Sourcebook (Live Oak Publications)

Working Together: Entrepreneurial Couples (Ten Speed Press/ Celestial Arts)

101 Easy Businesses You Can Start Now–Even If You're Just About Flat Broke (Dennis Weaver)

COURSES, SEMINARS, & SPEAKERS

This chapter contains additional resources for learning how to have a home business, including resource lists, as well as some very interesting training programs. The imagination is the only limitation to how many uses a person can find for these resources.

Art Instruction Schools, 500 South 4th St., Minneapolis MN 55415. (612) 339-8721. Home Study courses in drawing, studio techniques, painting, cartooning, and advanced illustration. Study to be an illustrator for books, fashion, editorial, or for advertising. Accredited by National Home Study Council.

Aubrey Willis School, 301 W. Indian School Road, Phoenix AZ 85013. (602) 266-3323. Home study course covers every phase of piano tuning and repairing. Cost is $500 with no tools; $550 with beginner tools. Accredited by the National Home Study Council.

Bicycle Repair of America, Inc., PO Box 24106, Minneapolis MN 55424. (612) 920-5900. This company teaches how to make your simple garage-tinkering into a profitable business. They have a complete business and training system to show you how to start. Either part-time or full-time, you can develop your own business. Their complete business system costs $495 and includes: a business system manual; a 400-page technical training manual with 960 illustrations; advertising and sales promotion materials; business forms start-up packet; tools and parts catalogs; telephone hot line for assistance; and 500 personalized business cards. For information, send $1.

A Business of Your Own, Business Publications and Services for Women, PO Box 210662, Nashville TN 37221-0662. (615) 646-3708. This is a multi-faceted service firm that specializes in business publications and services designed to assist women in starting and managing small businesses. Their published information will inspire you, motivate you, educate you, and help you grow and develop skills to manage your own business.The founder and chief writer of the organization, Millicent Gray Lownes, is a well-known small business authority. She has a B.A., a M.B.A., and a PhD. degree in Business Administration. She has written nationally published columns called "Entreprenuerially Yours."

The basic courses from this company are 13 comprehensive business start-up manuals. One of these courses is called "Starting a Home Based Business," $59.95 (plus $3 for shipping). It is a very thorough publication, covering such topics as "Managing Time & Stress," "Success Stories," marketing techniques, mail-order directories, examples of home-based businesses, "The Business Plan," "Personnel," "Sources of Funds," etc.

Other courses include, "So You're Thinking About Starting a Business—A Comprehensive General Start-up Manual," $49.95; "Starting a Secretarial Service," $59.95; "Starting an Antique Business," $59.95; "Starting a Day Care Center," $59.95; and more. Add $3 for shipping. MC and VISA accepted.

Color Me a Season, Inc., 1070-A Shary Circle, Concord CA 94518. (415) 676-9184. Offers home study in the new process of Color Analysis. Accredited by the National Home Study Council.

Computer Information Ltd., PO Box 60369, San Diego CA 92106. Send for free list of 100 best services to offer using your personal computer.

County Schools, Inc., 3787 Main St., Bridgeport CT 06606. (203) 373-6800. Bookkeeping home study. Accredited by National Home Study Council and Connecticut Commissioner of Education.

Forum Publishing Company, 383 E Main St., Centerport NY 11721. (516) 754-5000. 40 page "Books for Your Business" catalog which lists dozens of books and publications about mail order, importing, exporting, starting and expanding a business. Send $1 postage for catalog.

Gemological Institute of America, 1660 Stewart St., Santa Monica CA 90404. (213) 829-2991. This school currently teaches 15,000 from more than 50 countries in its Home Study Program. Over the years, 40,000 jewelers, hobbyists and others have studied with GIA. The courses include study about diamonds and their grading, gem identification, colored stone grading, pearls, jewelry design and display, jewelry sales, gemologist program. Accredited by National Home Study Council.

Hollywood Scriptwriting Institute, 1300 N. Cahuenga Blvd., Hollywood CA 90028. (213) 461-8333. Home study to learn scriptwriting for motion picture industry, TV, cable TV, and videocassette industry. Graduates have sold scripts to *Love Boat, Cagney &*

Lacey, Beauty & the Beast, Trapper John MD, Hunter, Knots Landing, Facts of Life, and more. Accredited by National Home Study Council.

Homespun Communications, 7274 W. Hoover Ave., Littleton CO 80123. (303) 973-8757. Provides a "Home-based Word Processing Resource Packet" that lists useful resources for those who wish to start a word processing business at home, $5 postpaid. The resources include handbooks, magazines, newsletters, associations, reports, and on-line information. Very useful.

Lifetime Career Schools, 2251 Barry Ave., Los Angeles CA 90064. (213) 478-0617. Want a home business but not sure how to start? These courses not only teach you a skill, but also give ideas how it can become a home business. Home study courses in: landscaping ($440), dressmaking ($405), flower-arranging ($480), and doll repair ($385). All programs accredited by the National Home Study Council. Each course is comprehensive and a certificate of proficiency is issued upon successful completion of the study. Free booklet on each course available.

Mail Order Success Seminar, PO Box 2525, La Mesa CA 92041. (619) 432-6913. Mail order expert Russ von Hoelscher (see Profit Ideas, Inc.) and Al Galasso present all day seminars in San Diego. They have over 35 years experience between them, and an impressive record of mail order success. Both own their own companies, as well as being involved in seminars, workshops, and consulting. Call or write for next dates.

Mellinger Company, 6100 Variel Ave., Woodland Hills CA 91367-3779. The Mellinger Company is famous for their successful mail-order business, and for teaching others how to do it successfully too! They offer almost 25,000 different imported products at wholesale (or better) prices. There's cosmetics, sports equipment, vitamins and medicines, clothing, tools, lawn and garden supplies, auto accessories, jewelry, crafts and hobby kits, gold coins, and much more! The company will also teach you how to make a profit selling these products. Their "Home Mail Order Import Business Plan" guides your every step. All you need to do is write and ask for their free report, "How to Import and Export" and they will rush the information to you along with a free sample import.

Modern Schools of America Inc., 2538 North 8th St, Phoenix AZ 85006. (602) 990-8346. Correspondence instruction for gun repair. Accredited by National Home Study Council.

National Association for the Cottage Industry, PO Box 14850, Chicago IL 60614. (312) 472-8116. Coralee Smith Kern is available as a speaker on the topics of home business and the cottage industry. She has been called "The national housemother of homework" by the Chicago Tribune. She is the owner-manager of the successful at-home business, "Maid-to-Order, Inc.," which has grown from a 2 to 460 employee company providing maid and party service in Chicago and its suburbs. She publishes the "Mind Your Own Business at Home" newsletter. She was selected 1983 Women in Business Advocate of the Year by the US Small Business Administration. She is the founder and director of this NSCI organization.

Her expertise is strong in many areas of home business, with special emphasis on the legal aspects, how to begin a home business, and how to network. Call or write for information about seminars, lectures, consulting, and speaking engagements.

National Career Institute, 2021 W Montrose Ave., Chicago IL 60618. Toll-free 1-800-621-0660. Train at home for numerous types of home businesses. They have bookkeeping & accounting course that you have use to start your own home bookkeeping business. Write or call the toll-free number for free information.

National Technical Schools, Home Study Division, 456 West ML King Jr Blvd, Los Angeles CA 90099-2026. Toll-free 1-800-223-8837. Computer career training at home. This can be extremely useful because many home business are now based on using the personal computer to earn money. Also available is home study for air conditioning, refrigeration, and heating; and appliance servicing. Accredited by National Home Study Council and National Association of Trade and Technical Schools. Write or call toll-free number for information.

NRI Schools, McGraw-Hill Continuing Education Center, 4401 Connecticut Ave NW, Washington DC 20008. NRI trains you right at home in two top-paying opportunity fields that are wide open for trained specialists: building construction or air conditioning, refrigeration, heating. No experience is necessary. This school starts you with the basics, then builds your knowledge and skill a step at a time, while adding practical hands-on training. You'll even get the tools you'll need in the business. These are both fields where you can build a business of your own with proper training and motivation. Established since 1914. Send for a free NRI catalog. Accredited by National Home Study Council.

Para Publishing, PO Box 4232, Santa Barbara CA 93140-4232. (805) 968-7277. For orders, call 1-800-PARAPUB. Learn how to sell more books from the person who teaches people how to be publishers! Dan Poynter, author of the famous *Self-Publishing Manual,* opens his hilltop home/office overlooking the Pacific just five times a year to serious publishers for a two-day publishing and book marketing seminar. This seminar is guaranteed to save you thousands of dollars and hundreds of hours. You will learn how to publish and promote quicker, easier, and with greater results. Write and ask for information.

See ad page 44.

Travel-Travel International, Wulff Road, PO Box N8341, Nassau, Bahamas. Toll free 1-800-662-SAIL. Offers a Cruise Travel training course and license. Price is $495 for complete in-home agency. Free phone consulting comes with the package. Free information—write or call toll-free number.

Writers Institute, Inc., 112 West Boston Post Road, Mamaroneck NY 10543. (914) 698-7488. Home study for writing training geared towards journalism, special features, articles, television, films, radio, dramatic writing, poetry, and fiction. Established 1925. Accredited by National Home Study Council and New York State Education Department.

HOME BUSINESS NEWSLETTERS & MAGAZINES

Barbara Brabec Productions, PO Box 2137, Naperville IL 60566. Barbara Brabec is the editor of the *National Home Business Report,* a national home business newsletter since 1981. She has appeared on national television programs, such as the Home Show on ABC. This quarterly publication is a valuable business aid and networking tool for anyone interested in the home business industry. Readers contribute advice and hard-learned success secrets. They tell what works for them, and what mistakes to avoid. The report always inspires and motivates its readers, while helping them toward greater success in business. There are special feature articles in each issue (for example, "How to Generate Radio and TV Interviews," "Optimism Increases Performance") plus regular departments that give industry news, letters from the readers, home business profiles, book reviews, and more. Subscription: $18 year (4 issues).

Copreneurs, PO Box 825, Belmont CA 94002. "Copreneurs" is a quarterly newsletter devoted to topics of interest to every couple who have made the decision to work together and regain positive control of their lives. It focuses on today's economic pioneers who are building a new kind of partnership based on trust, equality, sharing and intimacy between partners. Subscription: $15 for 1 year, 4 issues.

This organization is also the address for the National Association of Entrepreneurial Couples.

The Doula, PO Box 71, Santa Cruz CA 95063-0071. (408) 423-5056. This quarterly magazine's full title is The Doula: A Magazine for Mothers. The word "doula" is a Greek word meaning "to serve", and it has come to represent women who through history "mother the new mother." The magazine nurtures and empowers women in mothering their own children. It challenges current social/ technological attitudes be viewing mothering as a vitally important commitment: encompassing pregnancy, birth, breastfeeding, midwifery, homeschooling, and health.A sampling of past articles include: "Becoming a Parent: Postpartum Support;" "The Myth of Birthing Safely;" "Children's Books that Nurture and Nourish;" "The Value of Learning Handcrafts at an Early Age;" ""What is Wrong with Infant Formula." This magazine is also a good source to find current home businesses and to advertise a home business. Subscription: 1 year, $15 (4 issues). Sample issue $4.

The Front Room, 63 Starmond Ave., Clifton NY 07013. (Mail address: PO Box 1541, Clifton NJ 07015-1541.) (201) 773-4215. Publishes "The Front Room News" newsletter six times a year. This is a crafts marketing newsletter and contains information such as "Craft Shop Marketplace" that lists shops and catalogs that carry handcrafts. Also lists sales reps, shows, marketing tips, profiles of craftspeople and special reports. Subscription $24 per year; sample issue $4. This company also carries books and booklets, so check "Books" chapter also.

Home Business News, 12221 Beaver Pike, Jackson OH 45640. (614) 988-2331. This bimonthly newsletter is packed with moneymaking information. Articles by nationally-recognized home business experts appear in this publication, such as a recent article by Jo Frohbieter-Mueller, author of *Stay Home and Mine Your Own Business*. Regular information on current home business legal status, good places to sell and buy products, resources, book reviews, software news, and more. Subscription: $39 year, 6 issues. Foreign $48. This company also publishes books.

Homespun Communications, 7274 W. Hoover Ave., Littleton CO 80123. (303) 973-8757. Provides a "Home-based Word Processing Resource Packet" that lists useful resources for those who wish to start a word processing business at home, $5 postpaid. The resources include handbooks, magazines, newsletters, associations, reports, and on-line information. Very useful.

Mothering Magazine, PO Box 1690, Santa Fe NM 87504. (505) 984-8116. A special advertising section each month is "Home Business", and home businesses offer their products in this section. Subscription: 4 issues/ $15.

Mothers' Home Business Network, PO Box 423, East Meadow NY 11554. (516) 997-7394. This is an organization for mothers with home-based businesses. Membership includes subscription to the newsletter *Homeworking Mothers*. For sample copy of newsletter and information about membership, send $2 and large SASE.

NextStep Publications, 6340 34th SW, Seattle WA 98126-3148. (206) 938-2290. Publishes the *Home Business Advisor* newsletter bimonthly. This newsletter is very popular with many home-based businesses for its practical, timely advice and current ideas. This publication also incorporates ideas of how to integrate a home business with a growing family and your lifestyle. There are first-hand stories from other families who have changed their lives through home businesses and are happy in their new lifestyle. Recent articles include, "Survival Strategies," "People-Powered Businesses," "Transforming Your Relationship with Money," and "Fathering vs. Career." Display ads and classified ads available for home businesses—good place for home businesses with a national product. Subscription: $24 for 1 year (6 issues).

Opportunity Press, Inc., Suite 1405, 6 N. Michigan Ave., Chicago IL 60602. (312) 346-4790. Publishers of *Opportunity Magazine,* a monthly magazine for entrepreneurs with product ideas, mail-order information, motivating articles, profiles of successful businesses started on a shoestring, and many classified and display ads of products and services for sale. Subscription: 1 year, $15 (12 issues).

Para Publishing, PO Box 4232, Santa Barbara CA 93140-4232. (805) 968-7277. For orders, call 1-800-PARAPUB. Produces a newsletter called "Publishing Poynters" fill with tips and ideas for publishers and is mailed free to publishers around the world. Write and ask for free copy.

See ad page 44.

$mall Businessman's Clinic, 113 Vista del Lago, Scotts Valley CA 95066. (408) 438-1411. Publishers of $mall Businessman's Clinic, a monthly 4-page newsletter in a question-answer format concerning the questions most asked by small businesses and home businesses. Now in it's 18th year of publication. Subscription: $28 a year; $35 foreign (air mail).

Worksteader News, 2396 Coolidge Way, Rancho Cordova CA 95670. (916) 635-8764. Monthly newsletter for home businesses. Includes information about companies that hire work-at-home employees.

HOME BUSINESS ORGANIZATIONS

American Home Business Association, 397 Post Road, Darien CT 06820. 1-800-433-6361. National organization for home-based businesses. Membership offers a lot of services including office supplies discounts and group-rate insurance, as well as their newsletter.

Computer Information Ltd., PO Box 25130, 7040 Hawaii Kai Drive, Honolulu HI 96825. 1-800-528-3665. FAX (808) 395-1045. Besides their extensive catalog of books on how to develop a personal computer business, this company is also the source for Computer Entrepreneur's Association of America. This organization's purpose is to help fellow computer entrepreneurs make money through networking and information. Membership includes 12 issues of the CEAA Report, the entire CEAA membership list, and a free listing in the CEAA Quarterly. Price of membership is $72 per year.

Copreneurs, PO Box 825, Belmont CA 94002. This organization is the address for the National Association of Entrepreneurial Couples, an association for couples who have made the decision to work together and regain positive control of their lives. It focuses on today's economic pioneers who are building a new kind of partnership based on trust, equality, sharing and intimacy between partners. Membership includes the newsletter "Copreneurs," the newsletter for every couple who wish to put an end to separate lives and separate agendas.

Entrepreneurs of America, Suite 224, 2020 Pennsylvania Ave NW, Washington DC 20006. 1-800-553-3932. This organization (EOA) offers services and products that you receive through a resource network. They offer a special group rate on merchant VISA/ MC processing as low as 1.75% (with no set-up fees) plus transactions can be credited to your local bank within 24 hours. Also offers special EOA Gold MasterCard with member interest rates almost 2% below other leading card issuers.EOA Delaware Precious Metals Exchange give you opportunity to purchase gold and other precious metals with no sales tax. There's also member discounts on resources of interest to entrepreneurs, such as books, magazines, and other products. Members receive a free subscription to the "Entrepreneurs of America" newsletter. You don't have to be a business owner to join EOA. All you need is the "entrepreneurial spirit". Membership is $49.95 annually, tax deductible. Satisfaction guaranteed.

Mothers' Home Business Network, PO Box 423, East Meadow NY 11554. This is an organization for mothers with home-based businesses. Membership includes subscription to the newsletter *Homeworking Mothers*. For sample copy of newsletter and information about membership, send $2 and large SASE.

National Association for the Cottage Industry, PO Box 14850, Chicago IL 60614. (312) 472-8116. Members have access to special rates for group insurance, travel discounts, legal referrals, Toshiba discounts, Hertz discounts, McBee bookkeeping system discounts, education loan guarantees, bimonthly 16-page bulletin of practical tips, collection services, Harvard Medical School Health letter at 50% discount, credit union, and credit reports. The organization has a bibliography relating to self employment and home business. They are also putting together a list of experts in the cottage industry. Special committees include zoning, legislation watch dog, fund raising, publicity, newsletter, and conference. This organization is active in lobbying for laws protective of home industries, and against laws which may hinder them. They are always interested in hearing about such legislation, either local, state, or regional.

Their newsletter, "Cottage Connection," is part of membership. This bimonthly publication keeps track of legal updates on the cottage industry, announces events such as the fall home business show, and other topics of special interest. Membership rates to the association are: $45 individual, $300 corporate, $75 non-profit.

National Association for the Self-Employed, PO Box 612067, DFW Airport TX 75261. Membership to this organization offers discounts on services and equipment, travel and leisure discounts, and health-related optional benefits. Their publication, "Self-Employed America," published 6 times a year, is a 4-color newspaper. They also have a free business library of books. Membership is $48 annually.

MAILING LISTS FOR USE IN HOME BUSINESSES

Why are mailing list resources so important for home businesses? Because any home business with a national product will ultimately use some direct mail to market their product. Knowing where to get reliable and reasonably priced lists is very important.

Ad-Lib Publications, 51 N 5th St., Fairfield IA 52556-1102. (515) 472-6617. Toll-free for orders 1-800-624-5893. Sells lists of booksellers, book publishers, publicity resources for books, book wholesalers and distributors, book markets and services, and book printers. If you need a list related to marketing books, this company probably has it. Also, their book *Book Marketing Opportunities: A Directory* lists these same sources in print format. This book contains a chapter that tells about where to get mailing lists appropriate to book marketing, but these mailing lists can also be appropriate for marketing other types as products as well. For instance, the chapter on mailing list sources contains addresses for finding mailing lists on doctors, dentists, business executives, economics, agriculture, photography, sweepstakes contestants, military, consumers, senior citizens, schools, radio-TV stations, political donors, and much more. This very useful book is over 300 pages, sells for $19.95.

American Business Lists, Inc., 5707 E 86th Cir., Omaha NE 68127. (402) 593-4500. Sells lists of craft-related businesses, such as craft stores, hobby stores, toy stores, etc. If you have a product to sell to these types of businesses, these lists might offer a good way to reach that market.

B. Klein Publications, PO Box 8503, Coral Springs FL 33065. (305) 752-1708. Offers mailing list of 10,000 mail order and catalog houses, $45 per thousand names; list of 1400 US and foreign manufacturers, $100 whole list; list of 1400 mailing list houses, $100 whole list.

This company also publishes a directory called *Directory of Mailing List Houses*. Provides the names of more than 1400 mailing list specialists including brokers, compilers, management companies, cooperative mailers, card deck mailers, and more. Arranged geographically and fully indexed. 240 pages. $65.

Camera Ventures, Photomoney Division, PO Box 771, Lamar CO 81052. List of over 30,000 active photographers and camera enthusiasts, most of whom are interested in home business opportunities.

Home Business News, 12221 Beaver Pike, Jackson OH 45640. (614) 988-2331. Sells mailing lists of home business seekers, opportunity seekers, multilevel seekers, book buyers, advertisers, buyers of craft related items, Jeffrey Lant's book buyers, Owen Publishing book buyers, and computer owners. Prices are $50 per 1,000; minimum order 500.

JAMI Marketing Services, 2 Executive Drive, Fort Lee NJ 07024. (201) 461-8868. Manages mailing list of opportunity seekers compiled by *Opportunity Magazine*.

McAfee & Company, 1815 Carpenter St., Bridgeport TX 76026. (817) 683-3023. 1-800-654-5541. Sells lists of opportunity seekers. 200 sample names, $7. 500 for $10. 1,000 for $18. 100,000 for $750. Multi-level names and categories also available from $15 to $30 per thousand. Special order of 2,000 names for $27 of book buyers, jewelry, novelties, recipes, diets, catalogs, sports. Zip-sorted pressure sensitive labels. Accepts MC/ VISA, and American Express.

Mega Media Associates, Inc., PO Box 4255, Newport Beach CA 92661. (714) 673-2290. Specializes in mailing lists of opportunity seekers (people interested in starting their own business). They handle about 20 different lists (including the list from Profit Ideas, Inc.) and the lists vary in size from 10,000 to 200,000 names. They run about $70 per thousand names, and the minimum order is 5,000 names.

Megatrend Systems, 6012 Laurel Lane, Ste 2311, Willowbrook IL 60514. Offers mailing lists of opportunity seekers. Guaranteed 100% deliverable—25¢ refund for any undeliverables. Printed on computer-printed peel and stick labels, zip sorted. 200 names, $15. 500 names, $25. 1000 names, $40. 5000 names, $150.

National Association for the Cottage Industry, PO Box 14850, Chicago IL 60614. (312) 472-8116. Mailing list of this association is available for rent. Call (312) 472-8116 and ask for Coralee Kern or call (312) 382-4501 and ask for Wendy Hansen.

Norman Hill, PO Box 1560, Jensen

Beach, FL 34958. 1-800-554-LIST or (407) 334-5205. Fresh responsive names in hundreds of categories. Will supply the small use or beginner as well as the volume mailer. Computerized on labels and guaranteed. Write for details or call for consultation.

Para Publishing, PO Box 4232, Santa Barbara CA 93140-4232. (805) 968-7277. For orders, call 1-800-PARAPUB. This company maintains mailing list of magazines and newsletters with book review columns, book reviewers, newspapers with book review columns, book wholesalers, distributors and exporters, and more. Write and ask for mailing list information.

See ad page 44.

Parkway Businesses Services, PO Box 29, Hinesville GA 31313. Orders (912) 369-6692. Ask for information about their "Unicorn's List," a list of up to 125,000 people seeking multi-level marketing opportunities. Reasonable prices: 200 names, $25; 500 names, $50; 1,000 names, $75; 2,000 names $125; etc.

S. E. Ring Mailing Lists, PO Box 15061, Ft. Lauderdale FL 33318. (305) 742-9519. List of opportunity seekers that can be purchased in small quantities. 100 names for $13, 500 names for $55, 1000 for $90. Provided on pressure-sensitive labels; shipped within 5 days via first class mail. Accepts VISA/ MC orders.

DISTRIBUTORSHIPS, DEALERSHIPS, SALES REP OPPORTUNITIES, & PARTY PLANS AVAILABLE TO HOME BUSINESES

This is a very important chapter because it lists companies that work hand in hand with home businesses on a regular basis. It's comforting for some people starting on their own to work with a company that is nationally recognized. Many kinds of business situations are available, ranging from party plans where a person sells products to family and friends, to multi-level marketing opportunities, which seem to be tremendously popular types of home businesses. A wide variety of product lines are represented by these companies, everything from kitchenware to herbal products to cotton underwear to children's magazines.

American Home Academy, 2700 South 1000 West, Perry UT 84302. (801) 723-5355 or (801) 723-3307. Families can become distributors of "Brite Music" curriculum. The products include a line called "Standin' Tall" that is a character-building series stressing 12 topics such as obedience, honesty, forgiveness, courage, love, service, self-esteem, and more. This series uses a combination of booklets, puppets, audio cassettes, and colorful carry bag. Other products are educational puzzles, cassettes, and books. Topics include safety, parenting, metric system, and patriotism. These products are popular with homeschooling parents. Send SASE for information.

Amway Corporation, 7575 E Fulton Rd., Ada MI 49355. (616) 676-6000. Nationally known multi-level company. This company not only sells its famous line of soaps and cleaners as well as numerous other products, but also has special services to offer.

Avon Products, Inc., 9 West 57th St., New York NY 10019. (212) 546-6015. World famous organization of beauty products, personal care products, and jewelry uses representatives to sell its products locally. Home parties a popular way to sell these products.

BASCO, Business Advertising Specialties Corp., 9351 De Soto Ave., Chatsworth CA 91311-4948. Many options for home businesses.This company has been written up in a special feature for *Opportunity Magazine*. Offers a imprinting machine for specialty advertising items. It prints on plastic, wood, metal, ceramic, glass, and virtually any surface. It prints on flat, contour, round, irregular, and curved surfaces. This machine can print up to 400 items per hour. Or, if you prefer, you can buy their products wholesale and sell them retail. For instance, a money clip pocket knife (imprinted) that sells retail for $3.50 costs you only 75¢; an imprinted tape measure that retails for $2.40 costs you only 48¢. You can become a sales rep—taking special orders for imprinted items. Send for free literature.

B. Klein Publications, PO Box 8503, Coral Springs FL 33065. (305) 752-1708. Offers a book distributorship to home businesses. You sell their publications (business directories and reference books) using catalogs they supply. They print the catalogs with your name and address. You mail them and get the orders. Then you send them a check for the books less the discount and they will dropship the books directly to the customer. There are no franchise fees, but you are required to place a minimum order of their catalogs. Ask to see their "Directory Dealer Agreement" and a copy of the book catalog.

Chet Baker, Rt 1 Box 297, Van TX 75790. (214) 963-5133. The Bakers offer an extraordinary opportunity for home businesses. It's a business that requires no products to stock or carry around to try to sell, provides extra income every month for the rest of your life, and is connected with a major national corporation. It's called Network 2000® and is an opportunity for people to gain an income for simply getting customers to switch over to US Sprint® Tele-communications Services. For every customer you sign onto US Sprint, you receive a commission and will receive a percentage every month based on their monthly phone bills. It's something that will last and last, and all you need to do is sign them up once! This is one idea that sounds too good to be true, but is a real opportunity! Training literature is provided, at a reasonable fee. Call or write the Bakers today.

See ad page 70.

Company One, PO Box I, Angwin CA 94508. (707) 965-2714. Distributors are being sought for "The Amplified Pilgrim's Progress," a dramatization of the entire book, "Pilgrim's Progress," featuring seventy-five actors, original music and sound effects on six one-

hour cassettes in a four-color album. The language is simplified for easy understanding. This adaptation was produced by Jim Pappas, and is a great contribution to the preservation of literature.

See ad page 70.

Decent Exposures, 2202 NE 115th, #226, Seattle WA 98125. (206) 364-4540. This is a dynamic young company committed to producing cotton underwear of the highest quality at an affordable price. All items made from 100% cotton knit or 80% cotton velour. The line includes bras, camisoles, and underpants. These are women's products designed by women.They specialize in hard-to-fit women because they can offer custom fits. Camisoles come in a variety of colors and cost $22. Underpants come in a variety of colors and cost $7. Bras vary according to size and fabric. Party plan available for home business. Write for brochure and price list.

Discovery Toys, Inc., 2530 Arnold Drive, Ste 400, Martinez CA 94533. 1-800-426-4777. These high quality toys are distributed through nationwide network of trained Educational Consultants. You can become one of these consultants—full-time or part-time. Training provided. Write or call toll-free number for information.

Drakestone Publishing Company, PO Box 20873, Oklahoma City OK 73120. Offers dealerships for selling their manual "How to Get a Job with the US Government." This book is a 42-page booklet that retails for $10, but the company will wholesale for $2 to $5 depending on quantity ordered. There is a membership fee required. For sample copy, send $2.

Eagle's Nest Homes, Route 5, Highway 20 East, Canton GA 30114-1569. Territories available for dealers to sell Eagle's Nest Homes. These homes are round, panelized homes with pagoda roofs. The homes are computerized for fire protection, climate control, and for medical emergencies. Optional additions can be added to expand the system. This is an opportunity for an ambitious salesman because you can sell the home to a do-it-yourselfer who is able to do the construction himself. He saves thousands of dollars in construction costs, you make a hefty profit without even lifting a tool. Send for free information how to become an Eagle's Nest dealer.

Fuller Brush Company, 2800 Rockcreek Parkway, Ste 400, Kansas City MO 64117. (913) 599-6421. Famous line of home care and personal care products. $29 fee to start.

Grolier Inc., Sherman Turnpike, Danbury CT 06816. (203) 797-3500. You can be a sales representative of *Encyclopedia Americana* or of their other educational products. They provide training.

Hanover Shoe, Inc., 111 N. Forney Ave., Hanover PA 17311. (717) 637-6631. Independent sales representatives are sought for selling their line of shoes. This company is over 50 years old.

Health Essentials, PO Box 339, Ashland OR 97520. Toll-free 1-800-334-5543, touch 15 (24 hours). Distributors wanted for their Multi-Pure® state of the art water purifier. This product effectively removes toxic chemicals, lead, chlorine, and asbestos, keeping water pure for drinking. Guaranteed quality product. The startup investment is as low as $300, and they have a flexible marketing plan. Free information packet.

Health Network, 2329 13th St., Boulder CO 80302. (303) 443-3552. This young company sells two lines of herbal and nutritional products (Nature's Sunshine Products and Nanci Nutritional Products) and health-related books. All products available to the public retail, and also distributorships available. These are multi-level marketing plans.

Herbal International Formula for Health, Randy & Kip Gorder, 3200 Louise, Kingman AZ 86401. (602) 753-3602. Offers distributorships to sell a unique formula that will improve health. This formula has been helping people for years. Proven success. This energetic company will teach you everything you need to know to be a successful distributor. Write or call for free information.

Highlights for Children, Inc., 803 Church St., Honesdale PA 18431. (707) 233-1080. Independent sales representatives are the only way the children's magazine *Highlights for Children* is sold. It is not sold on newsstands and does not contain any advertising. Write to see if a dealership is open in your area.

Joyful Visions, PO Box 51, Guinda CA 95637. (916) 796-3435. Sells distributorships of several lines of products for vibrant energy through balanced living. They carry Sunrider International® (Sunergy, Vitalite, Kandesn lines of herbal formulas, weight managements programs, and personal care products); Matol Km® herbal formula; Cell Tech Super Blue Green Algae; V.E. Irons Products, Hydro Floss Plaque Control System; Multi-Pure Drinking Water System; Nature's Spring Water Purifier; Colema Board; and Japanese Life Sleep System. Multi-level marketing companies. All products guaranteed. Send for catalog.

Kirby Corporation, 14600 Detroit Ave., Cleveland OH 44107. (216) 228-2400. Sales reps are used to sell their vacuum cleaners. Write for information.

Klassicorp, USA, Inc., c/o Charles G. Austin, RD 1, Rt 19 South, Belmont

NY 14813. (716) 268-5735. Distributorships available for Watkins, Purity water filters, plus a simplified bookkeeping and tax systems, and a long distance discount phone service system. Full time or part time. Send $8.50 for complete details (complete enrollment included) or call for information.

Life Products, PO Box 620182, Newton MA 02162. (617) 964-5433. An independent Neo-Life Distributor. Sells a Water Dome home water purifier and Consolaire air filter (air purifier). Affordably priced. Also offers a complete line of home and industrial strength biodegradable cleaning products, personal care products, a safe weight loss and maintenance program, and organically derived nutritional supplements. 100% satisfaction guaranteed. Dealer inquiries welcome.

Mail Order Associates, 120 Chestnut Ridge Rd., Montvale NJ 07645. (201) 391-3660. Using their "Distinctive Gifts by Mail" catalog with your name printed on it, you can establish a home business. All you need to do it show the catalog to your customers, write up orders, and they will dropship the items directly to your customer. The merchandise is guaranteed and they promise to ship promptly. Products include such items as leather wallets, jewelry, bookends, personalized items, phone hearing aids, magnifiers, desk organizers, knives, travel items, and more. The products are useful household items, but unique. You need to be a member to buy their products wholesale. Membership costs $165 and can be charged on MC/VISA. Your wholesale purchases can also be charged. Send for their packet of information.

Marion C. Snipes, 2622 Boldt, Tyler TX 75701. (214) 597-5451. Sells Sunrider® products in her home business. The various product lines are: Sunergy (vitamins and supplements, herbal products); Naturalife nutritional supplements, Vitalite vitamins, Kandesn beauty products. She also offers distributorships for these lines. A distributorship kit is $35 (includes literature and video) and the distributor is required to buy $100 wholesale products. The distributor must sell $100 minimum to receive a commission check.

Mary Kay Cosmetics, Inc., 8787 Stemmons Freeway, Dallas TX 75247. (214) 630-8787. The representatives for Mary Kay Cosmetics are called beauty consultants and sales directors. Home parties are one way sales are made, as well as follow-up telemarketing. To start, a small investment is required.

Mason Shoe Mfg. Company, Chippewa Falls WI 54774. 1-800-826-7030. Earn up to $26 commission for each pair of shoes you sell from the Mason Shoe catalog. This catalog contains color photos of over 400 styles to choose from for men and women, sizes 4-16, widths AA-EEEE. Products guaranteed. You show the shoes, write the order, and collect the cash deposit. Dealers can also earn bonuses, extra cash, and prizes. Write or call toll-free number for free details.

Melaleuca, Inc., 560 Broadway, Idaho Falls ID 83402. (208) 522-0700. Melaleuca products from Australia including shampoo, soap, oils, hand creams, lip balm, cleansers, detergent, spot remover, industrial strength cleanser, automatic dish detergent. douche, ointments, breath fresheners, vitamins, amino acids, minerals, digestants, and more. These products sold through multi-level distributors.

Multi-Pure Drinking Water Systems, 9200 Deering Ave., Chatsworth CA 91311-5858. (818) 341-7577. Distributors wanted for their Multi-Pure® state of the art water purifier. This product effectively removes toxic chemicals, lead, chlorine, and asbestos, keeping water pure for drinking. Guaranteed quality product. Flexible marketing plan. Free information packet.

Nanci Corporation International, PO Box 701080, Tulsa OK 74170-1080. 1-800-825-8848. Multi-level distributorships available for their health care products.

Nature's Sunshine Products, Inc., PO Box 1000, Spanish Fork UT 84660. (801) 798-9861. Nature's Sunshine products—herbs, extract, bee follen, vitamins, minerals, supplements, oils and lotions, hair conditioners, beverages, snacks, personal care products, water treatment system, diet products, waterless cookware, and more. Sold through multi-level distributorships.

Write for information.

Neo-Life Company of America, PO Box 5012, Fremont CA 94537. (415) 651-0405. This national company offers distributorships for its cleaners and personal care products. Multi-level marketing.

Ness Studios, 83 Scarcliffe Drive, Malverne NY 11565. (516) 593-2410. Ness Studios has designed a method of turning a photograph into a hand-painted oil portrait. You can cash in on the idea without even being an artist. All you need to do is to represent them and sign up customers. For additional details, which include complete sales kit, a color print and selling aids, send $3 (refundable).

See ad page 74.

Oriflame USA, 76 Treble Cove Rd., North Billerica MA 01862. (508) 663-2700. Offers distributorships to women who would like to become beauty advisors and sell their lines of European skincare and bodycare products. Training is provided, and hours are flexible. Write for information.

The Pampered Chef, c/o Sue Rusch, 4600 Normandale Highlands, Bloomington MN 55437. (612) 893-9775. The Pampered Chef® is looking for demonstrators for their product line of high-quality kitchen tools. Products includes slicers, graters, pizza baking items, bread baking items, pan sets, cookie droppers, skillets, apple wedgers, pasta servers, fancy salad molds, cookware sets, ice shavers, cutting tools, and much more. Over half the products are under $10. This unique business opportunity allows you to be in business for yourself, but not just by yourself. You have the support of an experienced staff. You're not pressured, so you don't have to pressure your customers. Send for details.

See ad this page.

Photo-Craft of America, 1920 S Broadway, St. Louis MO 63104. This company has developed a truly unique product that you can sell through their party plan. All you do is get a photo from your customer, send it to the company with your order, and the company processes the photo into a hook rug kit. The company sends you a complete kit of rug canvas designed exactly like the photo, yarns, pattern, and even instructions. The photo is even returned intact. You're offering your customer a unique way to make a cherished heirloom. Send $1 (refundable) for a sales kit.

Premier Publishers, PO Box 330309,

Ft Worth TX 76173-0309. Phone orders (817) 293-7030. You can be a distributor of their books without even stocking them. They will dropship your order. There are thousands of books to sell in their catalog on subjects such as business, health, mail order, diet, cooking, new age, travel, how-to, children's, sports, hobbies, and more. They have special sales aids to help you sell professionally. There is a full satisfaction guarantee on all their books, and they expect their dealers to offer the same guarantee to their customers. The initial order is very small ($50 retail, $25 cost to you) so it's easy to get started. Send for their "Mail Order Dealer's Wholesale Book News."

Also, in their catalog of books they offer two good books on dropship sources: *Book Dealers Dropship Directory,* listing reliable dropship publishers and distributors, $11 postpaid; *American Drop-Shippers Directory,* 16th edition, listing companies that offer everything from heirlooms to sausage kits through dropshipping, $8 postpaid.

Profit Ideas, 254 E Grand Ave, Escondido CA 92025. (619) 432-8375. This company offers you the opportunity to be a distributor of their very successful line of entrepreneurial books. (Titles listed in chapter on books.) It's a very simple, yet effective, way to start being self-employed. Many people have done this and made significant profits. Also, by reading his books and learning his methods, you can learn the secrets of successful entrepreneurs. There is no gimmick, it's a real offer. To find out details, write and ask for their free publication, "How to Make $2,000 a Week Selling Information by Mail".

Purity 2000 Enterprises Inc., PO Box 26126, Akron OH 44319. (216) 376-9090. Distributorships available for Purity 2000® water filter systems. Several models of equipment available. Write for business opportunity information.

Regal Ware, Inc., 1675 Reigle Drive, Kewaskum WI 53040-0395. (414) 626-2121. Imperial® Air Cleaner, Imperial® Water System and the new Kitchen Nutrition® Cooking System to be marketed nationwide by in-home consultants. Excellent support programs and exclusive distributorships available. Write for information.

Royal Plastics, 2348 N Lindbergh, St. Louis MO 63114. (314) 426-4310. This is a plastic thermoforming company that offers distributorships to sell 3-D store front letters. These letters come in all sizes and colors, and custom styles or logos can be created. You can sell these to local businesses and earn a 50% commission with no investment. Write or call for information.

See ad page 76.

Roy Babineaux, 502 Evangeline Dr., Lafayette LA 70501-5534. (318) 232-1229. Mr. Babineaux represents a candy manufacturer that sells fudge and other homemade candies by mail. These candies are guaranteed fresh. He is responsible for selling dealerships for home businesses. Write to him for details.

Shaklee Corporation, Shaklee Terraces, 444 Market St., San Francisco CA 94111. (415) 954-3000. Independent distributors sell Shaklee's product lines of cosmetics, health care, household, and some services. Small investment to start. Multi-level operation.

Spotted Pony Creations, PO Box 219, Cochranville PA 19330. (717) 529-6256. Instructors of childbirth classes may write for brochures to distribute the products. Spotted Pony Diaper Bag/ Backpack, a unique cotton quilt diaper bag in vibrant colors, $36 postpaid. Also 100% cotton-knit baby washcloths, $4.50 for 6 or $8 for 12, postpaid. Waterproof nylon zippered stuff sack, 9" x 12", to use with damp baby cloths makes a good alternative to commercial baby wipes, $2.50 each or $7 for 3 postpaid. This company offers 10% discount to participants of childbirth classes. Free gift offered with all diaper bag orders. Money back guarantee on all products. Free brochure.

S & S Press, PO Box 5931, Austin TX 78763-5931."Amazing Reprints" is a series of 500 old-time how-to booklets, first published 1989-1948. Topics include alternate energy, farm, home, shop, lab, tools, hobbies, crafts, toys. Price range: $2 to $8. Satisfaction guaranteed. Dealer rates available upon request.

St. Anthony Messenger, 1615 Republic St, Cincinnati OH 45210. (513)

241-5615. The St. Anthony Messenger is a national Catholic family publication that's been published by the Franciscans for 96 years. It has over 400,000 circulation. This publication is circulated by independent agents from their home. This is a home business that offers generous commissions, bonuses, permanent work, and a protected territory.

Sunrider Corporation, 452 West 1260 North, Orem UT 84057. (801) 224-5271. Multilevel company that sells personal care products, health care products. (Sunergy, Vitalite, Kandesn lines of herbal formulas, weight managements programs, and personal care products).

Sylvan Eve Jewelry, 10 Bristol Way, New Castle DE 19720. (302) 323-0297. Toll-free 1-800-328-5383. This company wholesales jewelry. You can buy one piece of a thousand, there is no minimum order. They will even dropship to your customer, no extra charge. They offer 5 plans to choose from to help you get started in business. For $15, you get a starter kit that includes 5 catalogs(catalogs are full color, 36 pages of jewelry), complete paperwork, ring sizer, and free enrollment. For $25 you receive all of the above plus one sample jewelry item. A Profit Package is offered for $129, which include carry case with display boards, paperwork, plastic ring sizer, gift, and 9 items of jewelry. Additional sales aids available, such as jewelry boxes, ring displays, jeweler pins, jewelry cleaner, polishing puff. All items guaranteed.

Tender Fashions Inc., 19 Midstate Drive, Auburn MA 01501. The company is currently looking for dealers to sell their specially designed clothing to seniors in nursing homes and at home. They have unique clothing that fits the special needs of older people. Write for free details.

Tropicals, 11516 Pleasant Meadows Drive, Gaithersburg MD 20878. Through Tropical, you can sell exotic tropical seeds and develop a mail order business of your own. Write for information.

U.S. Safety & Engineering Corporation, 2365 El Camino Ave., Sacramento CA 95821. (916) 482-8888. Sales reps sell security systems for this company. Write for information.

V. Beaumont Import-Export, 184 Banning St., Thunder Bay, Ontario, Canada P7B 3J3. (807) 345-4462.Their line of fashion jewelry and eelskin leather items are available to distributors. One of their lines of jewelry is Paua Shell Jewelry, items made from abalone. Merchandise is guaranteed. This merchandise can be sold by independent distributors, full-time or part-time, through home parties, flea markets, etc. Information $1.

Watkins Inc., 150 Liberty St., Winona

MN 55987. Offers dealerships to sell its various product lines, including food (flavorings, seasonings, aloe vera juice and concentrate, salad dressing mixes); health products (vitamins, ointments, inhalants, salves, liniments, skin products, perfumes, deodorants); and cleaning products (air fresheners, floor wax, polish, carpet fresheners, detergents, fabric softener, toilet cleaner, insecticide, mouse killer); and other miscellaneous products like fire extinguishers and pet food supplement. Watkins guarantees its products, and offers its dealers bonuses such as vacations, jewelry, furs. It's a way to have a family business but still be associated with a respected organization. Start-up cost is only $59 to become part of this nationally recognized company.

Waterwise, Inc., PO Box 45945, Center Hill FL 33514-0459. (904) 787-5008. Toll-free 1-800-874-9028. Sells drinking water distribution systems. They offer toll-free consultation, floor displays, brochures, training manuals, visual aids, and will even dropship to customers. Exclusive territories offered to dealerships.

World Book Inc., 510 Merchandise Mart Plaza, Chicago IL 60654. (312) 245-3456. Independent sales reps sell the *World Book Encyclopedia* and other educational products. No charge for sales kit.

Zenith Advanced Health Systems, Inc., PO Box 1739, Corvallis OR 97339. (503) 754-7380. Toll free (outside Oregon) 1-800-547-2741. Multi-level marketing company that has several product lines: nutritional supplements, vitamins, skin care, adaptogens, minerals, proteins, clean air and water systems.

WHOLESALE PRODUCTS AVAILABLE TO HOME BUSINESSES

Many companies are eager to sell products wholesale to home businesses. They are looking for ambitious sales people to increase their market. Some will even provide dropshipping for their customers, which means that the wholesale company ships direct to the final customer. This saves the home business person the expense and trouble of receiving and then shipping products. Some companies also provide sales tools, such as catalogs, advertising brochures, and specialized display items.

A-1 Sunglass Import Company, 2289 Industrial Parkway West, Hayward CA 94544. 1-800-822-8090 (toll-free from outside CA.) Offers more than 200 different styles of sunglasses wholesale. Prices range from $6 to $24 per dozen. Color catalog available.

ACME Premium Supply Corp., 4100 Forest Park Blvd., St. Louis MO 63108-2899. (314) 531-8880. Orders 1-800-325-7888. Catalog full of flea market merchandise and novelties. Ever wonder where carnivals bought their stuffed animals and other prizes wholesale? Well, Acme's the place. They have hundreds of styles of stuffed animals from panda bears to flamingos to that dog (what's his name?) in the beer commercials. There's plastic mugs, glass goblets, satin dice on key chains, and more. These are good items to buy wholesale from them at Christmas time and sell at flea markets. There's also a lot of other toys and games wholesale, like dart boards, mini pocket games, yo-yos, water color sets, marking pens, plastic bracelets, etc. Send for their free 136 page full-color catalog, or call for a copy.

Allied Fashions of Rhode Island, Inc., 1088 Main St., Pawtucket RI 02860. (401) 725-2235. Sells engraved crystal pendants wholesale. The pendants are made from genuine Austrian crystal and are offered in a variety of initials. Each pendant comes attached to a card and sealed in an individual plastic bag. Price: $36 dozen (each pendant sells for $6 retail).

ANKA, 90 Greenwich Ave., Warwick RI 02886. Sells gold, silver and costume jewelry wholesale. Catalogs have over 3600 items. Send for two free catalogs.

BASCO, Business Advertising Specialties Corp., 9351 De Soto Ave., Chatsworth CA 91311-4948. Many options for home businesses. This company has been written up in a special feature for *Opportunity Magazine.* Offers a imprinting machine for specialty advertising items. It prints on plastic, wood, metal, ceramic, glass, and virtually any surface. It prints on flat, contour, round, irregular, and curved surfaces. This machine can print up to 400 items per hour. Or, if you prefer, you can buy their products wholesale and sell them retail. For instance, a money clip pocket knife (imprinted) that sells retail for $3.50 costs you only 75¢; an imprinted tape measure that retails for $2.40 costs you only 48¢. You can become a sales rep—taking special orders for imprinted items. Send for free literature.

Blimpy Floating Signs, Dept 33, Fishermans Road, Box G, Truro, Cape Cod MA 02666. (508) 487-3437. Giant Blimpy Signs can be seen for miles. They have hot air balloons and roof-top balloons. These are useful for home businesses and flea markets—check with local ordinances first. Send for free brochure and wholesale price.

Charles Merchandise, Inc., 1655 N Mannheim Rd., Stone Park IL 60165. (312) 344-8118. Orders toll free 1-800-445-7928. FAX (312) 344-8125. Quality sunglasses that they import. Examples: aviator/smoked, $6.50 doz; Miami Vice-style/ wayfare, $6.90 doz; sport/turbo, $9.90 doz. Other items include gloves, socks, baseball caps, fishing gear, knives, and calculators. Send $1 for catalog.

Chuck Moser Flag Company, 1081 S. Shore Drive, Parkville MO 64151. (816) 741-6827.Complete line of flags for sale—US, states, foreign, religious, military. They can even make specialty flags for corporations, organizations, or flags with advertising messages. They also sell banners, balloons (stock and custom made), flag poles, and flag hardware. Top quality products. Discounts for quantity makes this an opportunity for dealers.

See ad page this page.

Cook Bros, Inc., 240 N. Ashland, Chicago Il 60607. (312) 384-4664.

Importers and wholesalers. Full-color catalog full of brand-name merchandise. They sell wholesale products from Sharp ®, Sanyo®, Proctor Silex®, Texas Instruments® and other national brands. They also feature religious items, 14K jewelry, clocks, cutlery, tools, novelties, carded goods, and monthly specials. Send $1 for their current catalog (refundable with first order.)

Crayon Caps, PO Box 1809, Mendocino CA 95460. (707) 964-7549. Crayon Caps are a colorful solution for keeping small heads warm. The durable 100% cotton interlock fabric is colorfast and pre-shrunk. They are self-lined hats and designed to last. Great gifts for newborns and fun for toddlers and school-age kids. The company is a cottage-industry employing mothers who want to be at home and also earn income. Various sizes and colors; two styles. Caps $7.95 each plus $1.45 shipping for first hat (additional postage each additional hat). Send for brochure for additional information.

This company also sells wholesale and has a "home sales program" which enables you to buy caps at a discount for resale.

Creative Products Inc., 3400 E Century Ave., Bismarck ND 58501. This company has developed a product called SpringTime® that purifies water through a two-stage, water-cooled fractional distiller. You can develop your own home business selling and installing such a system. Send $3 for color brochure and wholesale prices.

Global Video, 2140 East 7th Place, #2, Los Angeles CA 90021. 1-800-736-3456. This company has a line of videos called "Children's Cartoon Classics," that feature Donald Duck, Daffy Duck, Bugs Bunny, Popeye, Superman, Tweety Bird, and other big name cartoon stars. Each tape has a running time of approximately 30 minutes. These videos are produced on top-quality 3M tape for superior durability. A sample pack of 50 bestsellers is $112.50. They guarantee fast, reliable daily service. Write for more details or call in your order on their toll-free number.

Lasting Impressions, PO Box 22065, Lake Buena Vista FL 32830. (407) 298-5866. Offers a spool of Diam-O-Last chain that you can use to make custom necklaces, bracelets, and ankle chains. These chains come on a 30-inch Lucite spool and cost from only 8¢ to 21¢ per inch. There is a lifetime guarantee on the chains. Orders filled within 24 hours. These chains can be sold at home parties, flea markets, fairs. Complete starter kit is $349 which includes everything you need including inventory, display, and tools. No special training is needed. For information about Lasting Impressions plus a sample piece of chain, simply write. For information plus a 7" golden nugget wrist chain, send $5.

Lorina's Creators of Glass, 7909 15th Ave., Brooklyn NY 11228. This shop creates individually hand-sculpted bell hearts trimmed with 21 K gold. The hearts are 5" high and 3 1/2" wide with a delicately crafted double glass and gold layered bell bell in the center while on top two doves with wings of layered gold are perched. High quality craftsmanship guaranteed. Wholesale prices are $12 each for 1 to 5 dozen (sells for $19.95 retail). For a sample demo send $14.95.

Mail Order Associates, 120 Chestnut Ridge Rd., Montvale NJ 07645. (201) 391-3660. Using their "Distinctive Gifts by Mail" catalog with <u>your name</u> printed on it, you can establish a home business. All you need to do it show the catalog to your customers, write up orders, and they will dropship the items directly to your customer. The merchandise is guaranteed and they promise to ship promptly. Products include such items as leather wallets, jewelry, bookends, personalized items, phone hearing aids, magnifiers, desk organizers, knives, travel items, and more. The products are useful household items, but unique. You need to be a member to buy their products wholesale. Membership costs $165 and can be charged on MC/VISA. Your wholesale purchases can also be charged. Send for their packet of information.

Mellinger Company, 6100 Variel Ave., Woodland Hills CA 91367-3779. The Mellinger Company is famous for their successful mail-order business, and for teaching others how to do it successfully too! They offer almost 25,000 different imported products at wholesale (or better) prices. There's cosmetics, sports equipment, vitamins and medicines, clothing, tools, lawn and garden supplies, auto accessories, jewelry, crafts and hobby kits, gold coins, and much more! The company will also teach you how to make a profit selling these products. Their "Home Mail Order Import Business Plan" guides your every step. All you need to do is write and ask for their free report, "How to Import and Export" and they will rush the information to you along with a free sample import.

Navajo Manufacturing, 5801 Logan St, Denver CO 80216. 1-800-525-5097. 20-page color catalog offering wholesale on sterling, turquoise, fashion jewelry, novelties, sunglasses, and displays. Catalog, $2, refunded with first order.

New Wave Sales, PO Box 87, Glenmoore PA 19343. (215) 384-6900. Toll-free 1-800-342-2250. Wholesaler of thousands of products including Harley-Davidson accessories, incense, potpourri, novelty items, and closeouts. All products unconditionally guaranteed. Catalog $1 (refundable).

Paris Perfumes, 764 E. Twain #20 C, Las Vegas NV 89109. Paris Perfumes manufactures imitations of expensive popular perfumes. These perfumes sell at a fraction of the cost of the originals, but it's almost impossible to detect the difference. You can be a dealer of these perfumes, and sell them at home parties or other ways.

Rokan Corp., Flexilok Division, 125-C Business Center Dr., Corona CA 91720. Sells a unique burglary-protection system called Flexilok. The system consists of a 10' vinyl coated steel cable, security plates, and a padlock. Put these on TVs, VCRs, stereos, etc, for added protection. Thieves would have to have both the time and tools to break the system—added security for your home! This system is available wholesale. For a sample demo system, send $34.95 ($49.95 retail) to the corporation.

Rose City Records, PO Box 13437, Portland OR 97213. (503) 282-1675. Producers of "A Labor of Love," an album of a collection of songs that show the joy and beauty of childbirth as a shared experience. Featuring singer/flutist Kate Finn and pianist Rick Weiss. The music's soothing quality and thoughtful lyrics make it an ideal gift for new or expecting parents. Reviewers have said about the music, "I was overwhelmed with the feeling of happiness and joy that came through." Cassettes, $11.95 postpaid; compact discs $15.95 postpaid. Wholesale prices available if you wish to distribute this music at classes, conferences, workshops.

Sheldon Cord Products, 2201 W. Devon Ave., Chicago IL 60659. (312) 973-7070. Orders 1-800-621-7999. Carries thousands of items and furniture. Examples: kid's sunglasses on cards, $18 gross; Miami Vice-style sunglasses, $6.90 doz; men's T-shirts, assorted, $10.90 doz; men's brown jersey gloves, $6.90 doz; rod and reel set, $7.90 set; baseball hats, assorted, $8.90 doz; ribbed ladies' tops, $4.90 ea; men's G-shock diver watch, $7.90 doz; diamond chip earrings, $12 doz; 33 mm camera, $3.50 ea; key chain calculator, $18 doz. Send $1 for catalog.

Snyder's Wholesale, RR 1 Box 120, Richland IN 47634. (812) 359-4296. Line of wholesale products includes rubber sunglasses ($13 doz), Chinese folding fans ($1.50 doz); magic knives ($2.75 doz); hair barrettes ($1.50 doz); and much more. Send $1 for catalog. $75 minimum order.

Specialty Merchandise Corp., 9401 DeSoto Ave., Chatsworth CA 91311-4991. This company has been written up in *Opportunity Magazine.* They have almost 3,000 products to choose from, such as luggage, hair styling sets, solid brass eagles, leaded glass lovebirds, marble desk penholder, jewelry rack, mug sets, cloisonne jewelry, gumball dispenser, burglar alarms, and much much more! Besides offering to sell at what they promise is "rock-bottom prices," they also show you how to use their dropshipping system and their party plan. They not only sell you the product cheap, but also teach you how to sell them to your customers! They offer a free book that shows over 21 ways to make money wholesaling.

Sylvan Eve Jewelry, 10 Bristol Way, New Castle DE 19720. (302) 323-0297.Toll-free 1-800-328-5383. This company wholesales jewelry. You can buy one piece of a thousand, there is no minimum order. They will even dropship to your customer, no extra charge. They offer 5 plans to choose from to help you get started in business. For $15, you get a starter kit that includes 5 catalogs(catalogs are full color, 36 pages of jewelry), complete paperwork, ring sizer, and free enrollment. For $25 you receive all of the above plus one sample jewelry item. A Profit Package is offered for $129, which include carry case with display boards, paperwork, plastic ring sizer, gift, and 9 items of jewelry. Additional sales aids available, such as jewelry boxes, ring displays, jeweler pins, jewelry cleaner, polishing puff. All items guaranteed.

Technology Services, 829 Ginette St., Gretna LA 70056. (504) 392-9239. Large line of surveillance, debugging, and personal protection product available. Technical assistance available on all kits.

Tropicals, 11516 Pleasant Meadows Drive, Gaithersburg MD 20878. Through Tropical, you can sell exotic tropical seeds and develop a mail order business of your own. Write for information.

Verma World Traders, PO Box 1424, Des Plaines IL 60017-1424. Special exotic brass ashtrays from India, shaped like a globe. Discount priced at $9 each for 1 to 5 dozen. (Retail $14.95 each.) Sample $9.95 postpaid.

Waterwise, Inc., PO Box 45945, Center Hill FL 33514-0459. (904) 787-5008. Toll-free 1-800-874-9028. Sells drinking water distribution systems. They offer toll-free consultation, floor displays, brochures, training manuals, visual aids, and will even dropship to customers.

West Coast International, 3912 Third Ave., San Diego CA 92103. (619) 297-8182. Wholesaler of a variety of products including an artificial chamois in three sizes (for sample send $3); gift items such as laser super lantern, auto inspection lamp; executive supplies such as mini-stationary set, magnetic address books, magnetic pens; and novel household products such as static duster, vegetable slicer. Sales aids available including a video tape. Samples of their products available for a reasonable price. Send for brochure.

World Distributors, 3311 West Montrose Ave, Chicago IL 60618. They offer an large selection of quality products, from 14K jewelry, to silver jewelry to 35 mm cameras, and more. Their catalog is $1 (72 pages) and their minimum order is $50.

TOOLS, EQUIPMENT, & SUPPLIES FOR HOME BUSINESSES

Sometimes starting a home business is just a matter of finding the right tool or specialized machine, such as button-making machines or donut machines or candle-making supplies. All of these and more are listed in this chapter.

Badge A Minit, 348 North 30th Road, Box 800, LaSalle IL 61301. (815) 224-2090. Buttons are proven money-makers at fairs, flea markets, conventions, etc. They're fast and easy to make. Starter kit only $29.96 plus $1.75 for shipping. Free for free catalog and idea book.

Badge Parts Inc., 2320 W Greenfield, Suite 118, Milwaukee WI 53204. (414) 645-7541. Sells button-making equipment and parts, all sizes, manual and semi-automatic. Promises same day delivery for any size order.

BASCO, Business Advertising Specialties Corp., 9351 De Soto Ave., Chatsworth CA 91311-4948. This company has been written up in a special feature for *Opportunity Magazine*. Offers a imprinting machine for specialty advertising items. It prints on plastic, wood, metal, ceramic, glass, and virtually any surface. It prints on flat, contour, round, irregular, and curved surfaces. This machine can print up to 400 items per hour. See also "distributorship" and "wholesale products" chapters. Has many offers for home businesses. Send for free literature.

Bathmasters, 1595 Miller Road, Imperial MO 63052. (314) 464-3242. Offers a complete package for starting a business repairing and refinishing porcelain bathtubs. They provide the equipment, the training, a license agreement, materials, and on-going technical support. This business can be started in your home or garage with a modest investment. Write for free details.

Blimpy Floating Signs, Dept 33, Fishermans Road, Box G, Truro, Cape Cod MA 02666. (508) 487-3437. Giant Blimpy Signs can be seen for miles. They have hot air balloons and roof-top balloons. These are useful for home businesses and flea markets—check with local ordinances first. Send for free brochure and wholesale price.

Case Equipment Inc., Case Complex, Rt 4, Turner ME 04282. Toll free 1-800-223-1596. This company offers several products that will help you start a home business. Subli-Color® helps you produce your own high quality color heat transfers. You can make T-shirts, caps, or anything printed on metals, clothes, acrylics, nylons, more. Glaze-Tech Heating Oven is an appliance that enables you to put heat transfers on dishes, glassware, cups, mugs, salt & pepper shakers, ashtrays, etc. Photo Xpress is a complete 1-hour mini-lab for reducing, enlarging, making business cards, passport photos, and more. You can write or call their toll-free number for more information.

Kimball Woodcarver Company, 2602 Whitaker St., Savannah GA 31401. Sells a high-performance machine that makes wood signs. No experience needed; full instructions to start your own business. Write for free details.

Lil' Orbits, Inc., 8851 Research Center, Minneapolis MN 55428. (612) 535-3833. They have machines that can help you earn money by making donuts. They can supply you with portable booths, vendor carts and mobile units. There are no franchise fees. Write for a free "Donuts to Dollars" booklet that tells everything you need to know.

Mr. Button Products, Box 68355, Indianapolis IN 46268. (317) 872-7000. Would you like to make and sell customized buttons? This company sells button machines, button parts for all machines sold in the US, and custom printed buttons. They're the button specialists! Write or call for details.

Parkway Businesses Services, PO Box 29, Hinesville GA 31313. Orders (912) 369-6692. This company will provide printing at a very reasonable cost. For instance, regular 8 1/2 by 11 letter size circulars run $55 for 3,000 one-sided and $115 two-sided. They also print envelopes, booklets, letterheads, do typesetting for ads and circulars, and print shipping labels.

This company also publishes periodically a 32-page catalog/advertising circular called "American Mail Marketing Guide" that contains useful information on companies providing home business opportunities and services. Also, this catalog has a list of printing services available from the company. This catalog might be a good place for home businesses to place advertising, if their products would be of interest to other home businesses or opportunity seekers.

Pourette Mfg Inc., 6910 Roosevelt Way NE, Seattle WA 98115. (206) 525-4488. FAX (206) 525-2795. Complete lines of candle and soap making supplies. Molds, dyes, wick, wax, scent, fading inhibitor, embossing tools, applied messages, holders and bases, instruction booklets. Candle and soap making has become very popular for home businesses. Send $2 (refundable) for their catalog.

Vinyl Industrial Products, Montrose, Chicago IL 60618. 1-800-621-0660. Provides a vinyl repair kit with materials and instructions (plus business guidance) that shows you to do vinyl repairs for car shops, motels, hotels, restaurants, clinics, offices, hospitals, schools—wherever there's a vinyl repair job to be done. Free information by writing or calling toll-free number.

HOME BUSINESSES

This section contains information about home businesses that have products to offer on a national level.

HOME BUSINESSES—FAMILY PRODUCTS

This chapter contains information about home businesses that have family products for sale, including homeschooling products. For more information about homeschooling, see the final pages in this book for books by Blue Bird Publishing.

American Home Academy, 2700 South 1000 West, Perry UT 84302. (801) 723-5355 or (801) 723-3307. Families can become distributors of or purchase "Brite Music" curriculum. The products include a line called "Standin' Tall" that is a character-building series stressing 12 topics such as obedience, honesty, forgiveness, courage, love, service, self-esteem, and more. This series uses a combination of booklets, puppets, audio cassettes, and colorful carry bag. Other products are educational puzzles, cassettes, and books. Topics include safety, parenting, metric system, and patriotism. These products are popular with homeschooling parents. Send SASE for information.

The American Home Academy is also the publisher of the book *Home School Decisions* by Joyce Kinmont. It deals with 22 educational and child-rearing issues, such as: How much time should a child spend at his desk? How should we socialize children? $6.95 plus $1 postage.

Blessingway, 321 Anawan St., Rehoboth MA 02769. Herbal preparations for the childbearing years. "Pregnancy Tea," a special blend of vitamin and mineral rich herbs containing red raspberry, comfrey leaf, nettles, and red clover flowers, $4.50 (30 servings). "Fertilitea," tea fortified with vitamins and minerals essential to female reproductive cycle, $4.50 (30 servings). Reusable tea bags, 3 per package, $1.20. "Diaper Rash Salve," herbs blended for their antibiotic and antifungal properties, $4.50 oz. "Belly Oil," a blend of herbs known for their anti-itch quality makes this a favorite for pregnant woman, $4.50/ 2 oz. bottle. Maternity T-shirts, extra, extra-large 100% cotton, front shows Blessingway logo—the radiant mother-to-be—

in royal blue on beige background, $7.50. "Nursing Tea," sweet, delicious blend of herbs to promote the mother's flow of milk, $4.50 (30 servings). More products in their free brochure; everything is priced under $8. Satisfaction guaranteed.

Decent Exposures, 2202 NE 115th, #226, Seattle WA 98125. (206) 364-4540. This is a dynamic young company committed to producing cotton underwear of the highest quality at an affordable price. All items made from 100% cotton knit or 80% cotton velour. The line includes bras, camisoles, and underpants. These are women's products designed by women.They specialize in hard-to-fit women because they can offer custom fits. Camisoles come in a variety of colors and cost $22. Underpants come in a variety of colors and cost $7. Bras vary according to size and fabric. Party plan available for home business. Write for brochure and price list.

Elaine Aldrich, RR 2 Box 2675, Westford VT 05494. (802) 879-4869. They offer a quarterly journal on Waldorf philosophy and other forms of holistic and spiritual parenting, schooling, and homeschooling. *Childhood: The Waldorf Perspective* is $20 for a year's subscription (4 issues) and $5 for a sample issue.

Home Centered Learning, PO Box 92, Escondido CA 92026. (619) 749-1522. A private supported educational unit helping parents helping their children learn.

Home Education Press, PO Box 1083, Tonasket WA 98855. (509) 486-1351. The *Home Education Magazine* is a well-rounded national homeschooling magazine. There is something for everyone in this publication. There are scholarly, yet readable articles about parental rights, ideas on developing curriculum, learning and teaching helps, book and product reviews, marketplace ads from national products, kid's pages, and more! Examples of articles: "Help! Where Can We Buy Textbooks?" by Donn Reed; "Back to Basics: Toys that have stood the test of time" by Stevanne Auerbach; "Developing an Art Curriculum" by Sherrie Ferrell.

What I especially like about this magazine is that it's for everyone. Within the homeschooling movement, some companies align themselves as strictly "Christian" or strictly "secular" and will have nothing to do with anything outside their particular viewpoint. However, this magazine has avoided aligning themselves on one side of the fence of the other, making a wonderful meeting place for all homeschoolers nationwide. Subscription: 1 year, 6 issues, $24. 6 month subscription, 3 issues, $12. Current issues, $4.50.

This company has many other homeschooling publications including one book called *The Home School Primer,* to help parents get started. 38 pages, $6.50 postpaid. *Home School*

• ***Home Education Magazine,*** published since 1983, is a bimonthly magazine for home schooling families. Each issue features major articles, news, regular columns, letters, resources, book and curriculum reviews, children's pages and more. Averages 48-56 pages per issue.

One year, 6 issues, $24.00 Introductory issue $2.50

"An excellent well-rounded national home schooling magazine"
Cheryl Gorder in The Home Education Resource Guide

"Home schooling from a variety of perspectives. Well-done, balanced coverage."
David and Micki Colfax, Homeschooling for Excellence

• **The Home School Primer**, updated annually, is a complete introductory guide to home schooling. **The Home School Primer** answers the most common questions people ask about this educational option, and presents over sixty reviews of home schooling books, publications, curriculums, and resources.

• **The Home School Primer**, 1989 Edition, 40 pages, 8 1/2" x 11", two-color cover, illustrated, detailed resource listings, indexed.

$6.50 postpaid

"The Home School Primer is a comprehensive introductory guide."
Cheryl Gorder in The Home Education Resource Guide

"Upbeat handshake to home schooling. Articles on "Why Homeschool?," "Does Home Schooling Really Work?," "Community Resources and Services," "Choosing a Curriculum." Your questions about socialization, legalities, support groups, college, and preschool education are also covered."
Mary Pride in The New Big Book of Home Learning

Special Home Business Distributor Discounts!
For more information write:

• Home Education Press • PO Box 1083, Tonasket, WA 98855

Reader is a collection of essays about homeschooling from some of the best writers on the subject. 164 pages, $12.75 postpaid.

See ad page 92.

Honeymoon Point, PO Box 124, Hope ME 04847. This is truly a unique company. It is owned by a 12-year-old homeschooled girl, Cara Green. She sells T-shirts that show some of the beauty of Maine summers that she has enjoyed at Honeymoon Point, the name of her grandparent's summer cottage. The T-shirts show the loon family with the caption, "When it comes to school there's no place like home!" Colors: light blue, red, teal and fuchsia. Sizes: adult S,M, L, XL; child S, M, L. Price: Adults $9. Child: $7. Add $1 shipping each shirt.

Mountain Meadow Press, PO Box 447, Kooskia ID 83539. (208) 926-4526. This home business publishes education-related books. *Home School: Taking the First Step* by Borg Hendrickson is a step-by-step guide through all components of a home school plan. There are clear and inclusive answers to your home school questions. Also includes up-to-date legal information for each state. Reading and resources directory includes. Over 300 pages, $14.95 postpaid. Brochure available.

The New Nativity Press, PO Box 6223, Leawood KS 66206. (913) 341-8369. Publishes homebirthing books. In *Birth and the Dialogue of Love,* by Marilyn A. Moran, a revolutionary but loving approach to childbirth is explained.$10.95. *Happy Birth Days* by Marilyn Moran is a collection of 50 personal accounts of birth at home the intimate husband/wife way. $11.95. Add $1.50 shipping first book, 50¢ each additional book. See the Home Business—Publications chapter for their homebirthing newsletter.

Poppyseed Press, 7490 W. Apache, PO Box 85, Sedalia CO 80135. (303) 688-4136. "Homeschool Writer" is a tri-annual publication for authors, editors, and self-publishers of homeschool literature. Writers share ideas, information, and questions on costs, sales, advertising, publicity, business philosophy, ethics, resources, writing, editing, publishing, and combining family and work. Send $6 with 3 SASEs.

Their book *College Admissions—A Guide for Homeschoolers* by Judy Gelner covers a topic of strong interest to people who are homeschooling—how their kids will successfully enter college. This author actually experienced having a senior who was entering college, and she gives glimpses of what it was like, such as: Was it frustrating? What can we expect? She also covers topics such as paperwork, testing, financial aid, and more. $8.95 postpaid.

The Wishing Stone, RD 3 Box 208, Washington NJ 07882. (201) 832-2901. Sells a collection of goods for the nurturing family. Their catalog consists of items such as 100% pure beeswax candles from $1.10 to $7.05; lamp candles from $9 to $42; Clear Light's Cedar Sachets from the mountain forests of New Mexico, 4 oz, $5 each; Cooperative games such as "Starwords," a challenging word game for the family, $11.50; *Dieting Your Way,* a manual for realistic diet plans, 41 pages, $4.50; Nature's Notecards, environmentally-sensitive hand-calligraphed notecards on recycled paper, several styles, set of 8, $5.25; *Non-Competitive Games Manual,* 60 page, $3.50; Hugs & Tickles game, $9; aprons with a message, various messages including "We're all one under the sun" and "let there be peace on earth and let it begin with me", child size, $8, adult size, $12; felt puzzles, such as alphabet soup with 24 felt pieces; books and more.

Something unique and special offered in this catalog is the "I Need Attention Please" pack of activity cards that encourage adults and children to share time in loving and constructive ways. 80 cards, $5.50.

They will also send you "A Kid's Catalog—For Kids...By Kids" by Rachel, the family's 12-year-old homeschooled daughter who has her own business. She sells Calling Cards, sets of business-card-size cards with designs such as endangered species or stuffed toys or fantasy creatures with lines for writing whatever the child desires. These are great educational items for kids, being able to emulate their role models, and also for just plain having fun. These cards are only $1.25 per set. She also sells Mystery Puzzles, which are puzzles within puzzles. Put the jigsaw puzzle together and you have a mystery and a game to play! Titles of the puzzles are: Case #1: Missing Treasure; Case #2: Moving Shadow; Case #4: Funny Footprint; Case #4: Howling Thing. Each puzzle is $3.75. Another product in the kid's catalog is bookmarks printed on 100% recycled paper. These bookmarks are 40¢ each.

Every item in the catalog has been used by this family and tested, so they are confident that they are providing high quality products for a fair price. They guarantee satisfaction. Write and ask for their catalog.

See photo page 104.

HOME BUSINESSES—CHILDREN'S PRODUCTS & TOYS

There are some very interesting and unusual children's and baby products available only through home businesses. These companies have developed a specialized niche in American business by providing products in demand by parents but not available through normal retail stores. Also, these companies are exhibiting a great concern for the environment by providing products that are environmentally sound. You will find that the quality of all of these products is superior and that the companies guarantee satisfaction.

Ampersand Press, 691 26th St., Oakland CA 94612. (415) 832-6669. Stimulating and fun educational card games on science and nature subjects. Products include "Predator," The Food Chain Game, (also available in French or Spanish), $7.95; "Krill," The Ocean Food Chain Game, $7.95; "The Pollination Game," shows interdependence of plants and animals, $7.95; "AC/DC," The Electric Circuit Game, $7.95; "Flowchart," The Game of Program Planning, $7.95; and more. Minimum shipping charge $2.75.

Baby Biz, PO Box 404, Eldorado Springs CO 80025. (303) 499-2469. Their motto is "Our Biz is Babies." Products include: "Diaper Covers" by Nikky, the Velcro® way to no-pin cloth diapering. Just lay a diaper on the Nikky and wrap it around the baby. No more plastic pants! Several styles from $6.50 to $12.50. "Baby Shades," to protect baby's eyes from sunshine while riding in the car. These shades stick to the window with static cling, no suction cups or adhesives. 13" by 22" reusable sheet. Only $4. "Di-D Klip" to use instead of diaper pins, 6 klips for $2.50. "Overall Stretchers," to make overall grow right along with your child, $4.50. Many more products, all of them satisfaction guaranteed. Send for catalog.

Comfey Carrier

Baby Care, PO Box 5620, San Mateo CA 94402. (415) 572-2689. Nursing pillow prevents backaches and strained arms by enabling the baby to be comfortably positioned snuggly against mother. Makes it easier for new mother to relax and nurse successfully. $27.45 postpaid.

Bumkins International Inc., 291 North 700 East, Payson UT 84651. (801) 465-3995. (801) 465-9330. Bumkins are waterproof, washable, all-in-one diaper liners. They come in baby and toddler sizes. No pins, not folding, soft and absorbent, environmentally safe. Sample diaper (baby size) $5.95. Sample diaper (toddler size) $7.95. Brochure available.

By Golly, Kit Clothes for Kids, PO Box 980011, Houston TX 77098-0011. This company sells kits that are pre-cut, ready-to-sew clothes made from first-quality, name-brand fabrics and notions. All notions necessary for completion are included in each kit, and if special tools are required, these are included also. Extra notions are included in case "something goes wrong." Basic philosophy behind the clothing design is that playclothes can be attractive and fun to wear while providing educational opportunities for the young wearer. Their present line focuses on counting and dressing skills: zipping, buttoning, snapping, tying and lacing. Items in the catalog include: "Activity Pockets," that are brightly colored specialty pockets in unique designs (dino egg, fish, peas in a pod) with zippers or buttons to teach special skills; "Smartie Pants," that are precut overall kits with activity pockets; cloth activity book with a collection of eight activity pockets. Pocket kits start at $4. Send for free information.

Colour Wheel Designs, 23158 Gonzales Drive, Woodland Hills CA 91367 or PO Box 8384, Calabasas CA 91372. (818) 704-1865. Colour Wheel Designs takes original children's art and duplicates it into T-shirts using only non-toxic fabric paints. Their unique process uses a combination of silkscreen and handpainting to capture the spontaneity of kid's creations. Parent just send their kid's artwork, and the original artwork is returned intact with the T-shirt. Prices run from $11.50 to $20 for T-shirts/ sweatshirts for children to adults. Discounts available for quantities. Each order contains washing instructions. Full guaranteed. Send for brochure.

Comfey Carrier, PO Box 447, Santa Cruz CA 95061. (408) 338-2017. Comfey is an Oriental-style baby-wrap that enfolds child and parents in snug comfort without stress to shoulders, neck or back. It can be worn in five different positions, each particular to progressive development stages from birth to three years old. Washable/ dryable. Sizes: Medium and Large. Price: $45 plus $3 shipping. Money back guarantee. Free brochure.

See photo opposite page.

Cot 'n Tot, PO Box 620159, Newton MA 02162. (617) 964-2686. They have "The Storybook Children's Wear Catalog." They offer a variety of natural fibers and accessories for children, birth through 10 years. Their sizing system makes ordering easy. Height and weight chart included. They ship anywhere within two business days, and offer giftgiving services. 100% satisfaction guaranteed. Items in the catalog include a classic hooded sweatshirt in choice of colors, $34; sweatdress in choice of colors, $44; floral party dress in shades of blue, green and lavender, $58; infant raglan shirt, various colors, $12; diaperaps® for ease of diapering, $7; fleece-lined canvas pants, very stylish, $22, much more.

Crayon Caps, PO Box 1809, Mendocino CA 95460. (707) 964-7549. Crayon Caps are a colorful solution for keeping small heads warm. The durable 100% cotton interlock fabric is colorfast and pre-shrunk. They are self-lined hats and designed to last. Great gifts for newborns and fun for toddlers and school-age kids. The company is a cottage-industry employing mothers who want to be at home and also earn income. Various sizes and colors; two styles. Caps $7.95 each plus $1.45 shipping for first hat (additional postage each additional hat). Send for brochure for additional information.

This company also sells wholesale and has a "home sales program" which enables you to buy caps at a discount for resale.

Dollies & Company, 931 Pearl St., Boulder CO 80302. (303) 444-8686. These exquisite handmade dolls open the child's imagination with their warm, engaging simplicity.These traditional dolls have been made for many years in Switzerland and Germany. They are based on the Waldorf philosophy. Natural fiber dolls, doll houses, furniture, doll clothes, wool balls, and silk capes. Girl doll, $85; boy doll, $80; elf doll, $36; baby bunting doll, $26.Shipping $4 first doll. Choices of skin color, hair color, eye color. Money back guarantee. Send for brochure.

See photo next page.

Dollies & Company

Elaine Aldrich, RR 2 Box 2675, Westford VT 05494. (802) 879-4869. Traditional children's clothing made from natural fibers. Wool coat, reminiscent of a more elegant era, 100% wool, in navy blue or dark brown. Runs $100 to $140 depending on size and on whether or not you want a hat/ hood. Bloomers, $16 to $20. Jumpers, blouses, dresses, and pinafores all available. $28 to $44. All from 100% cotton. Satisfaction guaranteed. MC/ VISA orders accepted. Because they are a cottage industry, they can make small changes in items ordered, and larger modifications can be made with special arrangements. They want to please you. Ask for their brochure with sample swatches.

They also offer a quarterly journal on Waldorf philosophy and other forms of holistic and spiritual parenting, schooling, and homeschooling. *Childhood: The Waldorf Perspective* is $20 for a year's subscription (4 issues) and $5 for a sample issue.

See photo next page.

Every Buddies Garden of Puzzles, PO Box 778, Corvallis OR 97339. This is a small family business dedicated to offering high quality, handcrafted, colorful children's puzzles that will last through many generations. There are about 25 designs to offer including "Peg Puzzles," with a peg on each piece for younger children; personalized name puzzles, and 3-D multi-layer puzzles. These puzzles are available wholesale to stores, galleries, and gift shops. Discounts available to churches and schools. A portion of their income is donated to an organization dedicated to a peaceful approach to problems in our world. Send for their full color catalog.

Figgy Pudding Music, 404C Via Rosa, Santa Barbara CA 93110. (805) 964-3066. Produces an audio tape called "Old Songs for New Children," 48 minutes of lively melody and harmony with songs such as "Old King Cole," "My Bonnie," "I Know an Old Lady," "Paw-Paw Patch," and more. This is traditional and folk music for the family and is charmingly arranged. Sung by Rebecca Wave. $10 postpaid.

Health Network, 2329 13th St., Boulder CO 80302. (303) 443-3552. This company sells two lines of herbal and nutritional products (Nature's Sunshine Products and Nanci Nutritional Products) and health-related books. Their catalog has a special family section with books and health products for pregnancy, children, nursing, etc. One of the books is a children's guide to understanding herbs. Another is a comprehensive parent's guide to herbs including information about childhood illnesses, first aid, nursing, and pregnancy. Newsletter available—one free issue offered to interested persons. Subscription: $8 a year, 4 issues. Distributorships available for the multi-level products.

Elaine Aldrich Company
100% wool coat for girls

Hugs for the Heart, Box 85, Rainbow Lake NY 12976. This company provides creative alternatives to society's intense focus on children's intellectual development at the expense of their emotional and spiritual aspects. Their products serve to stimulate your children's inherent gifts—spontaneity, intuition, imagination, creativity, curiosity, and cooperation. They offer a brochure containing several products priced from $2.95 to $50. Includes: "Exploring Right and Wrong," a beginner's guide to developing convictions about right and wrong on a personal level. Ages 8-15. $8.95. "Zen Blocks," 27 wooden silkscreened cubes with Japanese symbols for creative play (like 3-D dominoes.) Ages 6-adult, 1-13 players, $16. "Games Manual of Non-Competitive Games," over 170 games that require little or no equipment for cooperative play. Ages 3-12. $3.95. Please note that this organization donates 5% of their monthly profit to worthy non-profit organizations such as Habitat for Humanity, Sacred Hoop of American Resource Exchange, and Youth Ambassadors of America.

KMS Products, 741 South Burton, Arlington Heights IL 60005. (312) 259-4418. Has a catalog of self-improvement books that can be obtained for sending an SASE. This company also published a guide for the busy parent: *Managing Motherhood* by Marianne Seidenstricker. This booklet is a result of her experiences with three preschool children and offers practical advice and inspiration appropriate for a home-working parent. 40 pages, $4.95 postpaid.

See ad next page.

Kreations by Kristen, 9050 W. Waters Rd., Ann Arbor MI 48103. (313) 663-5909. "Baby Bunting"—sensitively handcrafted dolls made with 100% cotton fabric and stuffed with 100% virgin lamb's wool. Made from a deep concern and love of children to help children use their powers of imagination. $25. Also creators of "Country Bunting", $35, and "Holiday Bunting", $45. This company also has "100% Homegrown Baby" (that motto printed on) T-shirts and sweatshirts. Various sizes and colors. T-shirts, $5. Sweatshirts, $10. Send for brochure.

See photo next page.

Marvelous Toy Works, 2111 Eastern Ave., Baltimore MD 21231. (301) 276-5130. Their two catalogs offer durable toys made of the finest materials with no sharp edges, splinters, or breakable parts. All materials used are non-toxic. Creativity and imagination are encouraged by the use of these toys. Products include pine rocking horse, 14" high, 29" long, $30. Pine doll cradle, 12" by 24", $24. Limber Jack, a rhythm folk toy that originated in Appalachia, $13. People board, 16 "people" in four different colors sit on a 7" square maple board, unlimited uses, $6.50. Also puzzles, pull toys, lots of unit blocks, more. Satisfaction unconditionally guaranteed. Write for catalogs.

Metrobaby, PO Box 1572, New York City NY 10013-0869. Sells 100% cotton clothing and bedding for infants and toddlers. Creepers, daygowns, pants and overalls, bathrobes, custom diapers, nursing pads, etc. One of the especially cute products is a hooded infant robe made of terrycloth. Comes in two sizes, $18. All products fully guaranteed. Write for free brochure.

Kreations by Kristen
Bunting Dolls

My Little Owlet, 1 Dara Lane, Poughkeepsie NY 12601. (914) 462-1718. Several good products. "Baby's First Bunting Doll," Waldorf-inspired, natural fiber, 9" hooded, bright colors. $10 postpaid. The "Maine Baby Carrier®," to carry newborns in front, but can be changed to carry babies on the back too. Made of 100% cotton with padded straps and reinforced extra long ties. Blue color, machine washable. $36. "Toothpillow," the tooth fairy's secret helper. An 8" tooth-shaped pillow with a secret pocket for your child's tooth. 100% cotton bleached muslin with polyester fiber filling. The tooth is white but the pocket comes in red, blue and green. $4. "Baby's First Book," eight pages of 100% cotton in cheerful colors and patterns. Washable book. $9.50. "My First Colors & Shapes," a 7 x 7 book made of 100% cotton filled with brightly colored shapes, each shape has the name of the shape and its color stitched into the page. Washable. Can be personalized on the cover. $14.50. Personalizing $1.50 extra. "Count With Me," 7 x 7 counting book in 100% cotton. Washable. $22.50. Personalizing $1.50 extra. Add $1.50 postage for first item. Add $2 for shipping two or more items. Catalog available.

Papa Don's Toys, 87805 Walker Creek Rd., Walton OR 97490. (503) 935-7604. Original hardwood toys the incorporate color, movement, and sound. This family-owned business, started in 1973, makes original design toys that must meet high standard for play value, durability, and safety. All paints, oils, and materials are guaranteed to be non-toxic, non-splintering, and safe for teething. Stress points are reinforced. Their 16-page color catalog is full of treasures: roller rattle, $5; crib spinner, $14; pull-whale, $6.50; push rainbow maker (18 balls of six colors blend to create a rainbow when the toy is pushed, plus jingle bells for sound), $18; and everyone's favorite: rolling letters (wooden letter on wheels), $3 each. They guarantee satisfaction. Send for free catalog.

See profile page 27.

Parenting Insights, 87 Division Ave., Levittown NY 11756. (516) 731-7529. Publishes *The Rainy Day Survival Guide: Entertaining Activities for Two and Three Year Olds* by Jean M. Kaiser. Contains dozens of art, craft, and play ideas as an alternative to television. Activities includes things like: muffin tin toss, paper plate tennis, magnetic fishing. 78 pages, $8.95.

The Portland Soaker, PO Box 19827, Rochester NY 14619. (714) 624-5550.A 100% woolen diaper cover. It's soft, absorbent, preshrunk, custom fit without velcro, and available in plaids and solid colors.Sizes: newborn, 13-18 lbs, 18-23 lbs, 23-30 lbs. Soakers are $12 each. Kits that include fabric, elastic, and fully illustrated instructions are $9. Shipping minimum $1.50. Send for brochure.

Priority Parenting Publications, PO Box 1793, Warsaw IN 46580-1793. (219) 453-3864. "Priority Parenting" is a monthly newsletter designed to encourage and educate parents who believe in quality, natural childcare. Each month a different topic is explored through editorials, resources, personal experiences of parents across US and Canada plus opinions from a variety of childcare experts. Past topics have included: immunization, war toys, miscarriage, secondary infertility, and homeschooling. Trial subscription (6 months, 6 issues) $7. Full year subscription (12 months, 12 issues) $14.

This company also publishes *Not*

on the Newsstands, a resource book for parents, updated every 18 months, that lists over 150 publications for natural parenting and natural lifestyles, includes a section on working at home. Lists newspapers, newsletters, and magazines with their address, subscription costs, length, frequency, and basic philosophy. $12 postpaid.

A Real Doll, PO Box 1044, Sebastopol CA 95473. Kits for natural fiber dolls: 16" boy or girl, $28, 20" baby doll, $34, and bunting doll. Kits include booklet of detailed instructions, custom-dyed cotton knit with pattern silkscreened onto knit, washed and carded wool for stuffing, tubular gauze for inner head, cotton twine, thread, embroidery thread, natural fiber yarn, clothes patterns and instructions.Kits come in choices of hair color. "Minikits" available that include booklet of illustrated instructions, silkscreened pattern on knit, and tubular gauze for inner head. Other kits available for "Knitted Gnome," $14.80, and "Knitted Lamb," $14.80. Extra kits can be purchased for doll's clothes, beret kit, and natural straw sun hat. Brochure $1, includes fiber samples.

Rock-A-Bye Baby, HCR 21 Box 50, Washington VT 05675. (802) 883-5578. Innovative babycare items, such as "Comfey Carrier," which allows flexibility in adult's movement while carrying an infant, yet usable for children up to three years, $40. "Dove Tails," 100% biodegradable disposable diapers—all paper. 100 per case, small $19 per case, large $24 per case. "Rock a Crib," turns your crib into a soothing rocking cradle, easily. Fits all cribs with casters. $13.99. Shipping, add $3.50 minimum. Complete satisfaction guaranteed. Send for brochure.

Soaker Pattern, PO Box 3527, Wichita KS 67201. A make-it-yourself pattern offered for a cloth diaper cover. It is simply designed in four sizes and is ecologically and economically sound. $5.50.

Spotted Pony Creations, PO Box 219, Cochranville PA 19330. (717) 529-6256. Spotted Pony Diaper Bag/ Backpack, a unique cotton quilt diaper bag in vibrant colors, $36 postpaid. Also 100% cotton-knit baby washcloths, $4.50 for 6 or $8 for 12, postpaid. Waterproof nylon zippered stuff sack, 9" x 12", to use with damp baby cloths makes a good alternative to commercial baby wipes, $2.50 each or $7 for 3 postpaid. This company offers 10% discount to participants of childbirth classes. Instructors may write for brochures to distribute the products. Free gift offered with all diaper bag orders. Money back guarantee on all products. Free brochure.

The Virginia Puzzler, Rt 4 Box 243, Charlottesville VA 22901. (804) 978-7595. This company makes "Custom Photo Puzzles," where they turn an 8 x 10 photo into a custom cut puzzle mounted on masonite. Puzzles can be

Rachel Feinsod
A Kid's Catalog—For Kids...By Kids
Wishing Stone

This intelligent homeschooled young lady has a business of her own. She has a catalog called "A Kid's Catalog—For Kids...By Kids". She sells Calling Cards, which are business-card sized cards for kids. These calling cards each have a design such as endangered species or fantasy creatures, plus horizontal lines for writing. She also sells Mystery Puzzles, which are puzzles within a puzzle.

Homeschooling and home business often go hand-in-hand because many parents view learning how to make a living as an integral part of education.

Above: Zany Zoo Gang
Finger, hand & arm puppets in a wide variety of animals.

Left: The Virginia Puzzler
Turns an 8 x 10 photo into custom cut puzzle on masonite.

made from actual photo or from negative, and can be made into easy, medium, or difficult puzzles. Photo puzzles vary according to difficulty level wanted in the puzzle and according to whether you send a photo or a negative. "Name Puzzles," are colorful 3 1/2" letters with handles in 1 x 4 1/2" spruce. A color-matched bottom holds the letters in place. Turns into a coat rack as the child outgrows the puzzle. $2 per letter plus $3.50 for shipping. Money-back guarantee. Brochure available.

See photo opposite page.

The Wishing Stone, RD 3 Box 208, Washington NJ 07882. (201) 832-2901. Sells a collection of goods for the nurturing family. Their catalog consists of items such Cooperative games such as "Starwords," a challenging word game for the family, $11.50; *Non-Competitive Games Manual,* 60 page, $3.50; Hugs & Tickles game, $9; aprons with a message, various messages including "We're all one under the sun" and "let there be peace on earth and let it begin with me", child size, $8, adult size, $12; felt puzzles, such as alphabet soup with 24 felt pieces; books and more.

Something unique and special offered in this catalog is the "I Need Attention Please" pack of activity cards that encourage adults and children to share time in loving and constructive ways. 80 cards, $5.50.

They will also send you "A Kid's Catalog—For Kids...By Kids" by Rachel, the family's 12-year-old homeschooled daughter who has her own business. She sells Calling Cards, sets of business-card-size cards with designs such as endangered species or stuffed toys or fantasy creatures with lines for writing whatever the child desires. These are great educational items for kids, being able to emulate their role models, and also for just plain having fun. These cards are only $1.25 per set. She also sells Mystery Puzzles, which are puzzles within puzzles. Put the jigsaw puzzle together and you have a mystery and a game to play! Titles of the puzzles are: Case #1: Missing Treasure; Case #2: Moving Shadow; Case #4: Funny Footprint; Case #4: Howling Thing. Each puzzle is $3.75. Another product in the kid's catalog is bookmarks printed on 100% recycled paper. These bookmarks are 40¢ each.

Every item in the catalog has been used by this family and tested, so they are confident that they are providing high quality products for a fair price. They guarantee satisfaction. Write and ask for their catalog.

See profile of Rachel on facing page.

Zany Zoo Gang, PO Box 253, Randallstown MD 21133. (301) 655-1912. Creates lovable finger, hand, and arm puppets in a wide variety of animals. Priced from $5.50 to $30. 90 day guarantee, full refund or replacement. Will send brochure.

See photo opposite page.

HOME BUSINESSES—HANDCRAFTS

Elaine Aldrich, RR 2 Box 2675, Westford VT 05494. (802) 879-4869. Traditional children's clothing made from natural fibers. Wool coat, reminiscent of a more elegant era, 100% wool, in navy blue or dark brown. Runs $100 to $140 depending on size and on whether or not you want a hat/ hood. Bloomers, $16 to $20. Jumpers, blouses, dresses, and pinafores all available. $28 to $44. All from 100% cotton. Satisfaction guaranteed. MC/ VISA orders accepted. Because they are a cottage industry, they can make small changes in items ordered, and larger modifications can be made with special arrangements. They want to please you. Ask for their brochure with sample swatches.

See photo page 99.

The Herb Farm & Craft Company, PO Box 28, Parlin CO 81239. Herbal products and handcrafted gifts. "Herbal Hot Pads," cotton padded hot pads filled with their own special blend of potpourri, makes the kitchen smell great, $10 postpaid; "Sleepy Dreams," an herbal pillow filled with lavender flower, hop flowers, peppermint leaves, and their own blend of essential oils, with a lovely handmade cotton calico pillowcase edged in eyelet lace, choice of colors, $34 postpaid; "Simmering Scents," 2 oz drawstring bags with cinnamon sticks, cloves, allspice, star anise, sassafras bark, and orange peel, to add to a pot full of water, 4 bags for $12 postpaid. Also children's moccasins made of soft white deerskin for newborns or elkhide for larger sizes. Price varies with size. "Colorado Wild Mountain Wreaths," a very special holiday wreath made from products found only in the Rocky Mountains, from 13" ($30 ppd) to 21" ($50 ppd). More products found in their catalog.

KBS Designs, PO Box 844, Melrose MA 02176. This company sells hand embroidered sweatshirts done in a special punch embroidery. Designs include flowers, palm trees, rainbows, owls, clowns, balloons, lions, penguins, pandas, and sports figures. Sizes kids through adults. Prices range from $16 to $55. Send for free brochure. **See photo opposite page.**

KBS Designs
Hand Embroidered Sweatshirts

Kreations by Kristen, 9050 W. Waters Rd., Ann Arbor MI 48103. (313) 663-5909. "Baby Bunting"—sensitively handcrafted dolls made with 100% cotton fabric and stuffed with 100% virgin lamb's wool. Made from a deep concern and love of children to help children use their powers of imagination. $25. Also creators of "Country Bunting", $35, and "Holiday Bunting", $45. This company also has "100% Homegrown Baby" (that motto printed on) T-shirts and sweatshirts. Various sizes and colors. T-shirts, $5. Sweatshirts, $10. Send for brochure.

See photo page 101.

My Little Owlet, 1 Dara Lane, Poughkeepsie NY 12601. (914) 462-1718. Several good products. "Baby's First Bunting Doll," Waldorf-inspired, natural fiber, 9" hooded, bright colors. $10 postpaid. The "Maine Baby Carrier®," to carry newborns in front, but can be changed to carry babies on the back too. Made of 100% cotton with padded straps and reinforced extra long ties. Blue color, machine washable. $36. "Toothpillow," the tooth fairy's secret helper. An 8" tooth-shaped pillow with a secret pocket for your child's tooth. 100% cotton bleached muslin with polyester fiber filling. The tooth is white but the pocket comes in red, blue and green. $4. "Baby's First

Book," eight pages of 100% cotton in cheerful colors and patterns. Washable book. $9.50. "My First Colors & Shapes," a 7 x 7 book made of 100% cotton filled with brightly colored shapes, each shape has the name of the shape and its color stitched into the page. Washable. Can be personalized on the cover. $14.50. Personalizing $1.50 extra. "Count With Me," 7 x 7 counting book in 100% cotton. Washable. $22.50. Personalizing $1.50 extra. Add $1.50 postage for first item. Add $2 for shipping two or more items. Catalog available.

Papa Don's Toys, 87805 Walker Creek Rd., Walton OR 97490. (503) 935-7604. Original hardwood toys the incorporate color, movement, and sound. This family-owned business, started in 1973, makes original design toys that must meet high standard for play value, durability, and safety. All paints, oils, and materials are guaranteed to be non-toxic, non-splintering, and safe for teething. Stress points are reinforced. Their 16-page color catalog is full of treasures: roller rattle, $5; crib spinner, $14; pull-whale, $6.50; push rainbow maker (18 balls of six colors blend to create a rainbow when the toy is pushed, plus jingle bells for sound), $18; and everyone's favorite: rolling letters (wooden letter on wheels), $3 each. They guarantee satisfaction. Send for free catalog.

See profile page 27.

A Real Doll, PO Box 1044, Sebastopol CA 95473. Kits for natural fiber dolls: 16" boy or girl, $28, 20" baby doll, $34, and bunting doll. Kits include booklet of detailed instructions, custom-dyed cotton knit with pattern silkscreened onto knit, washed and carded wool for stuffing, tubular gauze for inner head, cotton twine, thread, embroidery thread, natural fiber yarn, clothes patterns and instructions.Kits come in choices of hair color. "Mini-kits" available that include booklet of illustrated instructions, silkscreened pattern on knit, and tubular gauze for inner head. Other kits available for "Knitted Gnome," $14.80, and "Knitted Lamb," $14.80. Extra kits can be purchased for doll's clothes, beret kit, and natural straw sun hat. Brochure $1, includes fiber samples.

Unicorn Clothing Company, 924 San Andres, Santa Barbara CA 93101. (805) 962-7048. Handcrafted camisoles and skirts. Catalog available.

Zany Zoo Gang, PO Box 253, Randallstown MD 21133. (301) 655-1912. Creates lovable finger, hand, and arm puppets in a wide variety of animals. Priced from $5.50 to $30. 90 day guarantee, full refund or replacement. Will send brochure. **See photo page 104.**

HOME BUSINESSES—HEALTH & BEAUTY PRODUCTS

Health Network, 2329 13th St., Boulder CO 80302. (303) 443-3552. This company sells two lines of herbal and nutritional products (Nature's Sunshine Products and Nanci Nutritional Products) and health-related books. Their catalog has a special family section with books and health products for pregnancy, children, nursing, etc. One of the books is a children's guide to understanding herbs. Another is a comprehensive parent's guide to herbs including information about childhood illnesses, first aid, nursing, and pregnancy. Newsletter available—one free issue offered to interested persons. Subscription: $8 a year, 4 issues. Distributorships available for the multi-level products.

Herbal International Formula for Health, Randy & Kip Gorder, 3200 Louise, Kingman AZ 86401. (602) 753-3602. Has a unique formula that will improve health. This formula has been helping people for years. This energetic company will also let you be a distributor of their product. Write or call for free information.

Joyful Visions, PO Box 51, Guinda CA 95637. (916) 796-3435. Sells several lines of products for vibrant energy through balanced living. They carry Sunrider International® (Sunergy, Vitalite, Kandesn lines of herbal formulas, weight managements programs, and personal care products); Matol Km® herbal formula; Cell Tech Super Blue Green Algae; V.E. Irons Products, Hydro Floss Plaque Control System; Multi-Pure Drinking Water System; Nature's Spring Water Purifier; Colema Board; and Japanese Life Sleep System. All products guaranteed. Send for catalog.

Life Essence, 3438 East Lake Rd., Suite 14-655B, Palm Harbor FL 35685. Natural health and beauty products featuring Aromatherapy Skin Care, Botanical Essence perfumes, bath oils, natural cosmetics, herbal hair and body care, gourmet bee pollen and more. Guaranteed. Send for free brochure.

Life Products, PO Box 620182, Newton MA 02162. (617) 964-5433. An independent Neo-Life Distributor. Sells a Water Dome home water purifier and Consolaire air filter (air purifier). Affordably priced. Also offers a complete line of home and industrial strength biodegradable cleaning products, personal care products, a safe weight loss and maintenance program, and organically derived nutritional supplements. 100% satisfaction guaranteed. Dealer inquiries welcome.

LOL Enterprises, 4282 W 10000 South, Payson UT 84651. (801) 465-4949. Offers natural and herbal products for health and beauty. Several lines of products are for sale. Melaleuca products from Australia including shampoo, soap, oils, hand creams, lip balm, cleansers, detergent, spot remover, industrial strength cleanser, automatic dish detergent. douche, ointments, breath fresheners, vitamins, amino acids, minerals, digestants, and more. Also sells Images products that lower cholesterol and blood pressure, help weight loss, increase energy, dissolve cellulite, tan skin. Also from Images: shampoo and conditioner, lash enhancer, skinny tip, mouth wash, facial moisturizer, body lotion. Another product line is Nature's Sunshine—herbs, extract, bee follen, vitamins, minerals, supplements, oils and lotions, hair conditioners, beverages, snacks, personal care products, water treatment system, diet products, waterless cookware, and more. They also carry Non-Scents, a volcanic mineral that absorbs odors and toxic gases. They also sell Matol Km. Send for information.

Marion C. Snipes, 2622 Boldt, Tyler TX 75701. (214) 597-5451. Sells Sunrider® products in her home business. The various product lines are: Sunergy (vitamins and supplements, herbal products); Naturalife nutritional supplements, Vitalite vitamins, Kandesn beauty products. She also offers distributorships for these lines. A distributorship kit is $35 (includes literature and video) and the distributor is required to buy $100 wholesale products. The distributor must sell $100 minimum to receive a commission check.

Simmons Pure Soaps, 42295 Hwy 36, Bridgeville CA 95526. (707) 777-3280, ext 6074. Since 1979, this family has been making soap on their farm in northern California. They also raise fruit, vegetables, poultry, goats, sheep, rabbits, cats, and children. They sell their homemade soap as well as bath salts, and yarns handspun from their sheep's wool. They display their wares at Crafts Fairs and offer these products through mail order. Types of soaps are: castile soaps, $1.35 each (various styles); vegetarian soaps, $1.35 each (various styles); mineral bath salts, half pound $3 (various scents); and bath accessories such as loofa scrubber, $1.50; 5" to 6" sea sponge, $3.50; natural bristle bath brush, $6.50; pumice stone, $1.50, and more. Ask for their brochure.

Towards Life Bodycare & Unique Products, PO Box 2243, Yountville CA 94599. (707) 944-0713. Natural cosmetics, made out of non-toxic herbs and oils. Send $2 for catalog.

Wind & Water, 1705 14th St., Ste 371, Boulder CO 80302. (303) 939-9356. The products and services in their catalog reflect their interest in the environment. They sell top-quality environmental monitoring and purifying devices including radiation meters, radon detectors for air, water, and soil, and air and water filters. Also offered are wind chimes, gem and flower essences, herbs, books, tapes (music of the Andes), environmental T-shirts, Comfey Carrier, and handcrafted Orion original sweaters. Their catalog has a unique feature: it has a resource section listing organizations with concern for the environment. Send for this unique catalog.

HOME BUSINESSES—MUSICAL PRODUCTS

Dreamsinger Harps, 3407 Arbor Rd., Lakewood CA 90712. (213) 421-4525. This home based company sells various kinds of harps. Celtic harps are lightweight, solidly built but with enough range to play, comfortable to hold, and made of oak. $300 to $400. Doorharps are to be attached to the inside of your front door and it sings to you when the door closes. Known in Sweden and Norway as a "Welkommen." Various styles, can be custom-styled, just $40 plus $2 shipping.

See ad next page.

Figgy Pudding Music, 404C Via Rosa, Santa Barbara CA 93110. (805) 964-3066. Produces an audio tape called "Old Songs for New Children," 48 minutes of lively melody and harmony with songs such as "Old King Cole," "My Bonnie," "I Know an Old Lady," "Paw-Paw Patch," and more. This is traditional and folk music for the family and is charmingly arranged. Sung by Rebecca Wave. $10 postpaid.

Harps of Lorien, 610 North Star Route, Questa NM 87556. (505) 586-1307. Makers of fine quality instruments for the whole family. The Lura-Harp®, Little Minstrel®, and Baby Minstrel®, harps are easy to play and will help to create a harmonious environment for your family. These harps run from $150 up.A catalog of these instruments, as well as music cassettes, Native American drums and flutes, records, percussion sets, door harps, guitars, pan pipes, Mid-West drums, music for pentatonic instruments, and more, is available free. Wholesale prices for stores and schools. Prices from $9 up.

See ad next page.

Rose City Records, PO Box 13437, Portland OR 97213. (503) 282-1675. Producers of "A Labor of Love," an album of a collection of songs that show the joy and beauty of childbirth as a shared experience. Featuring singer/flutist Kate Finn and pianist Rick Weiss. The music's soothing quality and thoughtful lyrics make it an ideal gift for new or expecting parents. Reviewers have said about the music, "I was overwhelmed with the feeling of happiness and joy that came through." Cassettes, $11.95 postpaid; compact discs $15.95 postpaid. Wholesale prices available if you wish to distribute

this music at classes, conferences, workshops.

Sound Creations, PO Box 912, Bisbee AZ 85603. (602) 432-7100. Sells flutes (side-blown diatonic in three styles, Shakuhachi Japanese end-blown medication flute, and bamboo pan flute in two styles); strings (psaltry, a simple harp of ancient design, and bowed psaltry, a chromatic Renaissance instrument); percussion (bamboo shakers, shekere, bamboo claves, rainstick); and kalimbas. Also has a bamboo flute instruction booklet. Send for catalog sheet.

See photos next page.

Products from Sound Creations

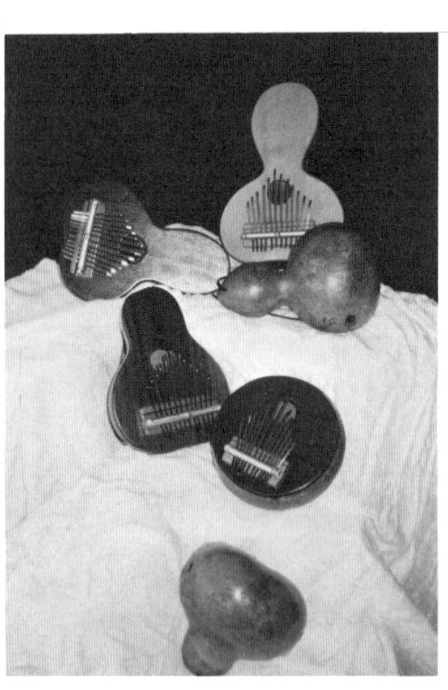

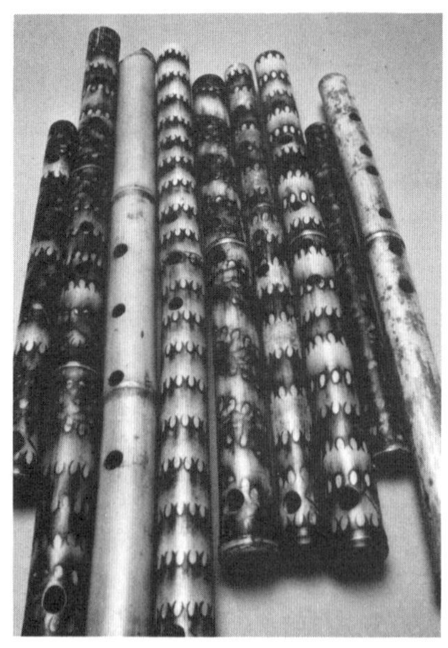

HOME BUSINESSES—PUBLICATIONS

The Doula, PO Box 71, Santa Cruz CA 95063-0071. (408) 423-5056. This quarterly magazine's full title is The Doula: A Magazine for Mothers. The word "doula" is a Greek word meaning "to serve", and it has come to represent women who through history "mother the new mother." The magazine nurtures and empowers women in mothering their own children. It challenges current social/ technological attitudes be viewing mothering as a vitally important commitment: encompassing pregnancy, birth, breastfeeding, midwifery, homeschooling, and health.A sampling of past articles include: "Becoming a Parent: Postpartum Support;" "The Myth of Birthing Safely;" "Children's Books that Nurture and Nourish;" "The Value of Learning Handcrafts at an Early Age;" ""What is Wrong with Infant Formula." This magazine is also a good source to find current home businesses and to advertise a home business. Subscription: 1 year, $15 (4 issues). Sample issue $4.

Elaine Aldrich, RR 2 Box 2675, Westford VT 05494. (802) 879-4869. They offer a quarterly journal on Waldorf philosophy and other forms of holistic and spiritual parenting, schooling, and homeschooling. *Childhood: The Waldorf Perspective* explores holistic and spiritual alternatives in parenting, on family life, cooperative initiatives, curriculum, imaginative play, the wonder of the natural world, storytelling, music, artistic work, handwork, festivals, reviews, resources, and networking. Helps nurture the magical time of childhood. Cost is $20 for a year's subscription (4 issues) and $5 for a sample issue.

See photo page 99.

Great Stuff Studios, 6617 Portsmouth Lane, Raleigh NC 27615. (919) 846-2961. The main service of this home-based business is designing logos, offering marketing advice, writing brochures and other publicity items for home-based businesses. However, they also offer twelve reports of interest to those investigating the possibility of starting a home business. They offer a brochure listing these reports for a long SASE. Ask for their "Publications for Small and Home-Based Businesses." Topics of these reports include: "How to create a brochure even if you have no money and no art skills," $3; "Planning for a better newsletter," $2; "But what can I do at home?" $2; "Selling calligraphy," $1.50.

Health Network, 2329 13th St., Boulder CO 80302. (303) 443-3552. This company sells two lines of herbal and nutritional products (Nature's Sunshine Products and Nanci Nutritional Products) and health-related books. Their catalog has a special family section with books and health products for pregnancy, children, nursing, etc. One of the books is a children's guide to understanding herbs. Another is a comprehensive parent's guide to herbs including information about childhood illnesses, first aid, nursing, and pregnancy. Newsletter available—one free issue offered to interested persons. Subscription: $8 a year, 4 issues. Distributorships available for the multilevel products.

Home Education Press, PO Box 1083, Tonasket WA 98855. (509) 486-1351. The *Home Education Magazine* is a well-rounded national homeschooling magazine. There is something for everyone in this publication. There are scholarly, yet readable articles about parental rights, ideas on developing curriculum, learning and teaching helps, book and product reviews, marketplace ads from national products, kid's pages, and more! Examples of articles: "Help! Where Can We Buy Textbooks?" by Donn Reed; "Back to Basics: Toys that have stood the test of time" by Stevanne Auerbach; "Developing an Art Curriculum" by Sherrie Ferrell.

What I especially like about this magazine is that it's for everyone. Within the homeschooling movement, some companies align themselves as strictly "Christian" or strictly "secular" and will have nothing to do with anything outside their particular viewpoint. However, this magazine has avoided aligning themselves on one side of the fence of the other, making a wonderful meeting place for all homeschoolers nationwide. Subscription: 1 year, 6 issues, $24. 6 month subscription, 3 issues, $12. Current issues, $4.50.

This company has many other homeschooling publications including one book called *The Home School Primer,* to help parents get started. 38 pages, $6.50 postpaid. *Home School Reader* is a collection of essays about homeschooling from some of the best writers on the subject. 164 pages, $12.75 postpaid.

See ad page 92

KMS Products, 741 South Burton, Arlington Heights IL 60005. (312) 259-4418. Has a catalog of self-improvement books that can be obtained for sending an SASE. This company also published a guide for the busy parent: *Managing Motherhood* by Marianne Seidenstricker. This booklet is a result of her experiences with three preschool children and offers practical advice and inspiration appropriate for a home-working parent. 40 pages, $4.95 postpaid. **See ad page 101.**

The New Nativity, PO Box 6223, Leawood KS 66206. (913) 341-8369. Quarterly newsletter for do-it-yourself homebirth couples. So far they have printed over 200 personal homebirth experiences by couples who have birthed in an intimate, loving way in the dimly-lit seclusion of their bedrooms. Includes book reviews. 1 year subscription, $10, 4 issues.

Parenting Insights, 87 Division Ave., Levittown NY 11756. (516) 731-7529. Publishes *The Rainy Day Survival Guide: Entertaining Activities for Two and Three Year Olds* by Jean M. Kaiser. Contains dozens of art, craft, and play ideas as an alternative to television. Activities includes things like: muffin tin toss, paper plate tennis, magnetic fishing. 78 pages, $8.95.

Priority Parenting Publications, PO Box 1793, Warsaw IN 46580-1793. (219) 453-3864. "Priority Parenting" is a monthly newsletter designed to encourage and educate parents who believe in quality, natural childcare. Each month a different topic is explored through editorials, resources, personal experiences of parents across US and Canada plus opinions from a variety of childcare experts. Past topics have included: immunization, war toys, miscarriage, secondary infertility, and homeschooling. Trial subscription (6 months, 6 issues) $7. Full year subscription (12 months, 12 issues) $14.

S & S Press, PO Box 5931, Austin TX 78763-5931."Amazing Reprints" is a series of 500 old-time how-to booklets, first published 1989-1948. Topics include alternate energy, farm, home, shop, lab, tools, hobbies, crafts, toys. Price range: $2 to $8. Satisfaction guaranteed. Dealer rates available upon request.

HOME BUSINESSES—SPECIALTY ITEMS

Canvas Crafters, 1705 14th St., #122, Boulder CO 80302. (303) 494-3807. Toll-free order number 1-800-365-1199. Hanging canvas chairs are made in Boulder by Bob and Diane. The chairs were a first place winner in the International Canvas Furniture Design Competition. They are carefully crafted with quality materials. They can be hung from a ceiling joist or outside from a porch rafter or tree branch. The chair is fully adjustable and comes ready to hang with hooks included. Price of adult chair, $59; footrest, $15; child chair, $39. Choices of fabric colors. Shipping $4.50 per order. MasterCard and Visa orders accepted.

See special profile on page 17.

Chuck Moser Flag Company, 1081 S. Shore Drive, Parkville MO 64151. (816) 741-6827. Complete line of flags for sale—US, states, foreign, religious, military. They can even make specialty flags for corporations, organizations, or flags with advertising messages. They also sell banners, balloons (stock and custom made), flag poles, and flag hardware. Top quality products. Discounts for quantity makes this an opportunity for dealers.

See ad page 81.

Great Stuff Studios, 6617 Portsmouth Lane, Raleigh NC 27615. (919) 846-2961. The main service of this home-based business is designing logos, offering marketing advice, writing brochures and other publicity items for home-based businesses. However, they also offer twelve reports of interest to those investigating the possibility of starting a home business. They offer a brochure listing these reports for a long SASE. Ask for their "Publications for Small and Home-Based Businesses." Topics of these reports include: "How to create a brochure even if you have no money and no art skills," $3; "Planning for a better newsletter," $2; "But what can I do at home?" $2; "Selling calligraphy," $1.50.

Homeopathic Educational Services, 2124 Kittredge St., Berkeley CA 94704. (415) 653-9270. Distributor of homeopathic books, tapes, medicines, and home medicine kits. They provide materials for beginners or medical professionals. Send SASE for catalog.

Homespun, PO Box 3338, Fairfield CA 94533. (707) 428-1345. Homespun is in the business of producing chair pad pillows. This company pays work-at-home sewers to produce these pillows. For each 36 pillows you sew, they pay $48. They supply the material (you pay a refundable deposit) and pay the postage. As you submit your finished work, the company pays you and ships you more supplies. You are required to purchase a non-refundable starter kit for $29.50 which includes a sample pillow, fabric, zipper, piping, the pattern, and complete instructions plus quality control list.

See ad this page.

Information Plus, 3189 Brennans Rd., Loomis CA 95650. Publishes "The American Do It Yourself Will Kit" for people to design their own wills. $10.95, completely guaranteed and refundable. Send for their free brochure, "Do I Need a Will?"

Into the Wind, 1408 Pearl St., Boulder CO 80302. Their catalog is truly unique: it is a full color catalog, 80 pages, of kites and kite accessories. There's every imaginable type of kite: sharks, flamingos, dragons, parrots, bats, cars, sky train, ghost clipper ship, Disney characters, Japanese style, box style, crystal style, and more. All in vibrant colors. Every accessory imaginable is there: wind meters, kite lights, kite anchors, kite parachute, kite packs, kite books, paint-a-kite kit, kite tape and kite parts. These kites make wonderful gifts.Send for this wonderful catalog.

L & M Marketing & Consultation, 1122 South 680 West, Payson UT 84651. (801) 465-3995. This company is a home-based business that is offering their expertise to help other home-based businesses get off the ground. They individualize their marketing advice for each client.

Technology Services, 829 Ginette St., Gretna LA 70056. (504) 392-9239. Large line of surveillance, debugging, and personal protection product available. Technical assistance available on all kits.

COMPANY DIRECTORY

A-1 Sunglass Import Company, 2289 Industrial Parkway West, Hayward CA 94544. 1-800-822-8090 (toll-free from outside CA.) 80

Aames-Allen Publishing, 1106 Main St., Huntington Beach CA 92648-2719. (714) 536-4926. 33

ACME Premium Supply Corp., 4100 Forest Park Blvd., St. Louis MO 63108-2899. (314) 531-8880. Orders 1-800-325-7888. 80

Acropolis Books, Ltd., 2400 17th St., NW, Washington DC 20009. (202) 387-6805. 33

Ad-Lib Publications, 51 N 5th St., Fairfield IA 52556-1102. (515) 472-6617. Toll-free for orders 1-800-624-5893. 65

Allied Fashions of Rhode Island, Inc., 1088 Main St., Pawtucket RI 02860. (401) 725-2235. 80

American Business Lists, Inc., 5707 E 86th Cir., Omaha NE 68127. (402) 593-4500. 65

American Home Academy, 2700 South 1000 West, Perry UT 84302. (801) 723-5355 or (801) 723-3307. 68, 90

American Home Business Association, 397 Post Road, Darien CT 06820. 1-800-433-6361. 63

Ampersand Press, 691 26th St., Oakland CA 94612. (415) 832-6669. 95

Amway Corporation, 7575 E Fulton Rd., Ada MI 49355. (616) 676-6000. 68

ANKA, 90 Greenwich Ave., Warwick RI 02886. 81

Art Instruction Schools, 500 South 4th St., Minneapolis MN 55415. (612) 339-8721. 55

Aubrey Willis School, 301 W. Indian School Road, Phoenix AZ 85013. (602) 266-3323. 55

Avon Products, Inc., 9 West 57th St., New York NY 10019. (212) 546-6015. 68

Baby Biz, PO Box 404, Eldorado Springs CO 80025. (303) 499-2469. 95

Baby Care, PO Box 5620, San Mateo CA 94402. (415) 572-2689. 96

Badge A Minit, 348 North 30th Road,

PRODUCT INDEX

This index lists the products found in all the chapters except the book chapter, because there is a separate book index at the end of that chapter. This index lists the products alphabetically with the company selling the product followed in parenthesis. Sometimes the product and the company name are the same. Sometimes a product has more than one distributor, and all the distributors are listed with their page numbers.

MORE BOOKS FROM BLUE BIRD PUBLISHING

ORDER FORM ON PAGE 144

Dr. Christman's LEARN TO READ BOOK
by Dr. Ernest Christman

A complete learn-to-read program for all ages. This highly illustrated book is a fun, yet effective way to teach anyone to read. Step-by-step the book uses the best building blocks for learning how to read.

ISBN 0-933025-17-3 256 pages $15.95

ORDER FORM ON PAGE 144

The Sixth Sense

Practical Tips for Everyday Safety
By Joseph Niehaus

Safety Tips For:

- ✔ Senior Citizens
- ✔ Students
- ✔ Employees
- ✔ Families

These tips require:

No special training

No special background

"If there is just one book all citizens should read—this is the book."—James M. O'Dell, Chief of Police, Kettering, Ohio.

"I believe that this is an important book. I heartily recommend it."—Clyde S. Morgan, Police Captain, retired, Kettering, Ohio.

OTHER BOOKS BY BLUE BIRD PUBLISHING

REAL DAKOTA!

REAL DAKOTA! is a book that celebrates the Dakota Centennial in a very special way—it focuses on the people who have made the states strong. It is a unique book about Dakotans—by Dakotans themselves.

The book shows more than the fact that Dakotans are a talented group of people. It shows that they are people with feelings similar to those of any group of people in the world—that is, universal emotions. They are compassionate, hard-working, patriotic, sensitive, and fun-loving. They have their weaknesses, but they are always working towards making things better.

And most of all, Dakotans are striving towards better communications between people, bridging the gaps between cultures and ethnic groups.

ISBN 0-933025-07-6 $11.95

WHO'S WHO IN ANTIQUES

edited by Cheryl Gorder

The only national comprehensive directory of the antique profession! It includes auction companies, show promoters, independent antique dealers, antique mall dealers, periodicals, appraisers, services, authors, publishers, and organizations. Well-organized reference.

ISBN 0-933025-10-6 $14.95

Order form on page 144

MORE BOOKS BY BLUE BIRD PUBLISHING

HOME SCHOOLS: AN ALTERNATIVE

by Cheryl Gorder

Explores the controversies of homeschooling and offers guidelines for parents interested in the alternative. Lists resources and home school organizations. Numerous reviews have applauded the book, including the nationally recognized *Booklist* and *Small Press Review*. The author has been on a national tour of radio and television interviews. She is also in demand by home school groups as a lecturer. Two months on the Small Press Bestseller list. Updated 1987.

ISBN 0-933025-10-6 $11.95

HOME EDUCATION RESOURCE GUIDE

by Don Hubbs

Hundreds of important addresses for home schooling materials and resources. Updated 1989. Includes resources for: legal information about home education; correspondence courses; textbooks; educational toys, games, & software; Bible education materials; child-training books; how-to-home-school books; help for the handicapped students and parents; home business ideas; home school support groups; speakers & seminars; audio-visual materials, and more!

ISBN 0-933025-12-2 $11.95

ORDER FORM

To order more books from Blue Bird Publishing, use this handy order form.

______	*Homeless! Without Addresses in America*	$11.95
______	*Education for Life*	$9.95
______	*Sharing Nature with Children*	$6.95
______	*Home Schools: An Alternative* (3rd edition)	$11.95
______	*Home Education Resource Guide* (revised)	$11.95
______	*Spacedog's Best Friend*	$6.95
______	*Home Business Resource Guide*	$11.95
______	*Dr. Christman's Learn-to-Read Book*	$15.95
______	*The Sixth Sense: Practical Tips for Everyday Safety*	$11.95
______	*They Reached for the Stars!*	$11.95
______	*Parents' Guide to Helping Kids Become "A" Students*	$11.95
______	*Home School Manual*	$15.50

Shipping Charges: $1.50 for first book.
Add 50 cents for each additional book.
Total charges for books: ______
Total shipping charges: ______
TOTAL ENCLOSED: ______

Checks, money orders, and credit cards accepted
NAME: ______
ADDRESS: ______
CITY, STATE, ZIP: ______

Please charge my _____ VISA ____ MasterCard
Card# ______
Expiration Date: ______
Signature: ______
Phone#: ______

Send order to:

BLUE BIRD PUBLISHING
1713 East Broadway #306
Tempe AZ 85282
(602) 968-4088